MAJO

POCKET BATTLEFIELD GUIDE TO

D-DAY

NORMANDY LANDING
BEACHES

- US AIRBORNE & UTAH BEACH
- POINTE DU HOC & OMAHA BEACH
- BAYEUX & GOLD BEACH • JUNO BEACH
- SWORD BEACH • BRITISH AIRBORNE

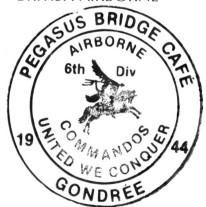

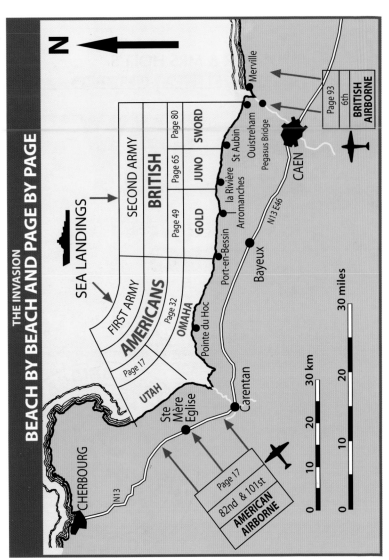

THE INVASION
BEACH BY BEACH AND PAGE BY PAGE

N

SEA LANDINGS

AMERICANS
FIRST ARMY

BRITISH
SECOND ARMY

Page 17

Page 32

Page 49

Page 65

Page 80

UTAH

OMAHA

GOLD

JUNO

SWORD

AMERICAN AIRBORNE
82nd & 101st
Page 17

BRITISH AIRBORNE
6th
Page 93

CHERBOURG

Ste Mère Eglise

Carentan

Pointe du Hoc

Port-en-Bessin

Arromanches

la Rivière

St Aubin

Ouistreham

Merville

Pegasus Bridge

Bayeux

CAEN

N13

N13 E46

0   10   20   30 km

0   10   20   30 miles

(Right) *Gen de Gaulle Memorial, Courseulles.*

MAJOR & MRS HOLT'S
POCKET BATTLEFIELD GUIDE TO

D-DAY

NORMANDY LANDING BEACHES

- US AIRBORNE & UTAH BEACH
- POINTE DU HOC & OMAHA BEACH
- BAYEUX & GOLD BEACH • JUNO BEACH
- SWORD BEACH • BRITISH AIRBORNE

LE 6 JUIN 1944
LES FORCES ALLIÉES
LIBÈRENT L'EUROPE

ICI

A COURSEULLES
LE 14 JUIN 1944
CHARLES DE GAULLE
LE LIBÉRATEUR
RETROUVE
LA TERRE DE FRANCE

Tonie and Valmai Holt

Pen & Sword
MILITARY

By the same authors:

Picture Postcards of the Golden Age: A Collector's Guide
Till the Boys Come Home: the Picture Postcards of the First World War
The Best of Fragments from France by Capt Bruce Bairnsfather
In Search of the Better 'Ole: The Life, Works and Collectables of Bruce Bairnsfather
Revised edition 2001
Picture Postcard Artists: Landscapes, Animals and Characters
Stanley Gibbons Postcard Catalogue: 1980, 1981, 1982, 1984, 1985, 1987
Germany Awake! The Rise of National Socialism illustrated by Contemporary Postcards
I'll be Seeing You: the Picture Postcards of World War II
Holts' Battlefield Guidebooks: Normandy-Overlord/Market-Garden/Somme/Ypres
Visitor's Guide to the Normandy Landing Beaches
Battlefields of the First World War: A Traveller's Guide
Major & Mrs Holt's Concise Guide to the Ypres Salient
Major & Mrs Holt's Battle Maps: Normandy/Somme/Ypres/Gallipoli/MARKET-GARDEN
Major & Mrs Holt's Battlefield Guide to the Ypres Salient + Battle Map
Major & Mrs Holt's Battlefield Guide to the Normandy D-Day Landing Beaches + Battle Map
Major & Mrs Holt's Battlefield Guide to Gallipoli + Battle Map
Major & Mrs Holt's Battlefield Guide to MARKET-GARDEN (Arnhem) + Battle Map
Violets From Oversea: Reprinted 1999 as Poets of the Great War
My Boy Jack?: The Search for Kipling's Only Son:
Revised limpback editions 2001, 2007, 2008, 2009
Major & Mrs Holt's Concise, Illustrated Battlefield Guide to the Western Front – North
Major & Mrs Holt's Concise, Illustrated Battlefield Guide to the Western Front – South
Major & Mrs Holt's Pocket Battlefield Guide to Ypres & Passchendaele
Major & Mrs Holt's Pocket Battlefield Guide to The Somme 1916-1918

First published in Great Britain in 2009 and reprinted in 2012 and 2015 by
Pen & Sword MILITARY
an imprint of
Pen & Sword Books Limited
47 Church Street, Barnsley, South Yorkshire, S70 2AS

Text copyright © Tonie and Valmai Holt, 2009, 2012, 2015
website: www.guide-books.co.uk

ISBN: 978 1 84884 079 9

Typeset in 8.5pt Optima by Pen & Sword Books Limited
Printed and bound in India by Replika Press Pvt. Ltd.

For a complete list of Pen & Sword titles please contact
Pen & Sword Books Ltd, 47 Church St, Barnsley, S. Yorkshire, S70 2AS, England
email: enquiries@pen-and-sword.co.uk • website: www.pen-and-sword.co.uk

CONTENTS

List of Itinerary Maps

Introduction

In a 15 miles deep strip behind the landing beaches there are almost 500 memorials and the straight line distance from one end of the beaches to the other is over 60 miles. To do any sensible justice to what there is to see requires at least 5 days in France. Most people do not have that time. We have been guiding travellers around the battlefield areas, or writing about them, for over 30 years and in this book we have put together simple itineraries that reflect not just the type of visitor but also the visits most requested by them – the 'highlights', as it were. This guide is practical rather than comprehensive.

Thus this Pocket Guide is designed for several different types of visitor -

- For those who wish to visit the D-Day beaches with just enough information to know broadly what happened where and what are the most important features to see
- For those with limited time at their disposal
- For those on a conducted tour wishing to prepare for their trip
- For those whose visit will be taken in an armchair at home

A very much more detailed guide book is our *Major and Mrs Holt's Battlefield Guide – Normandy D-Day Landing Beaches* which comes complete with a detailed map showing all the beaches and memorials, which those who would like to go into more depth about the historical background and to see more of the battlefield areas and their memorials, may wish to read. This volume is in effect a concise précis of the latter but, being reprinted more frequently, may be marginally more up to date.

When we conducted our first tour to the D-Day beaches there were no signed routes and only three major museums – Bayeux, Arromanches and Ste Mère Eglise. Today there are museums seemingly everywhere competing with each other for the tide of visitors.

In the 1970s the battlefield visitor was generally a veteran, perhaps with family members, or someone with a specific interest in visiting the grave of a relative, or in militaria. Now the general tourist to Normandy may well spend a day in looking at the beaches or visiting a museum or two as part of a normal Summer holiday and this book is intended to help them too.

A visit to Normandy without a guide, whether a book or a person, will result in much wasted time and frustration. It is also sensible to take a good map. Michelin and IGN produce modern road maps and our *Major and Mrs Holt's Battle Map of Normandy* shows where all the memorials, museums, battle lines etc are. A little preparation can add so much to a tour. An up-to-date GPS system can also be very useful and we have given lat and long references for the key sites, but back up your navigation with a map.

During your tour you will be travelling through an historic area, in places of outstanding beauty, with a reputation for delicious local products. We hope you have enough time to enjoy them. The Tourist section at the end of this book will give you some practical information on how to do so.

If you are fortunate during your visit you may see a venerable gentleman wearing a blazer with a pocket badge and perhaps a chestful of medals. He is almost certainly a proud member of the Normandy Veterans Association. If you are in the American area then that 80+ years old visitor will probably be wearing a side hat covered in badges. Go to them, shake them by the hand and say, 'Thankyou'.

Tonie and Valmai Holt
Woodnesborough, Spring 2009

About the Authors

Respected military authors Tonie and Valmai Holt are generally acknowledged as the founders of the modern battlefield tour and have established a sound reputation for the depth of their research. Their *Major & Mrs Holt's Battlefield Guides* series comprises without doubt the leading guide books describing the most visited battlefields of the First and Second World Wars. They have a unique combination of male and female viewpoints and can draw upon well over a quarter of a century's military and travel knowledge and experience gained in personally conducting thousands of people around the areas they have written about.

The authors with some of their books.

Valmai Holt took a BA(Hons) in French and Spanish and taught History. Tonie Holt took a BSc(Eng) and is a graduate of the Royal Military Academy, Sandhurst and of the Army Staff College at Camberley. They are both Fellows of the Royal Society of Arts and Science and have made frequent appearances on the lecture circuit, radio and television.

In December 2003 the Holts sponsored and unveiled a memorial to Capt Bruce Bairnsfather (the subject of their biography, *In Search of the Better 'Ole*) at St Yvon near 'Plugstreet Wood'.

In 2007 an updated edition of their biography of John Kipling, *My Boy Jack?*, was published to coincide with the ITV drama, *My Boy Jack*, starring Daniel Radcliffe and they acted as consultants for the IWM Exhibition of the same name.

In 2009, the 50th Anniversary year of the death of the cartoonist Bruce Bairnsfather, they updated their 1978 published collection of his 'Best' cartoons, *The Best of Fragments from France*, in conjunction with their publishers Pen and Sword MILITARY. All royalties from the sale of the book will go to the 'Help for Heroes' Charity.

For more information and latest news VISIT THEIR WEBSITE:
www.guide-books.co.uk

Abbreviations

Abbreviations used for military units are listed below. At intervals the full name of a unit is repeated in the text in order to aid clarity. Other abbreviations and acronyms are explained where they occur.

AB	Airborne		Gren	Grenadier
ABMC	American Battle Monuments Commission		Indep	Independent
			Inf	Infantry
AEAF	Allied Expeditionary Air Force		LCVG	Landing Craft Vehicle and gun
Armd	Armoured		LCVP	Landing Craft Vehicle and Personnel
Bde	Brigade			
BEF	British Expeditionary Force		LEC	*Liberté, Egalité, Citoyenneté* Mem
Bn	Battalion			
Brig	Brigadier		Lt	Lieutenant
Can	Canadian		LZ	Landing Zone
Cdo	Commando		Maj	Major
Cdr	Commander		Mem	Memorial
C-in-C	Commander-in-Chief		MoH	Medal of Honour
Civ	Civilian		Mus	Museum
Col	Colonel		NTL	*Normandie Terre-Liberté* totem
Com Deb Mon Sig	*Comité du Débarquement Monument Signal*			
			OP	Observation Post
Coy	Company		Para	Parachute
Cpl	Corporal		Pfc	Private First Class
CWGC	Commonwealth War Graves Commission		PIR	Para Inf Regiment
			Prov	Provisional
DD	Duplex Drive		Regt	Regiment
Div	Division		RM	Royal Marine
DSC	Distinguished Service Cross		RV	Rendezvous
DZ	Dropping Zone		Sgt	Sergeant
Eng	Engineer		SGW	Stained Glass Window
FOO	Forward Observation Officer		SOP	Standard Operational Procedure
Fr	French			
GC	George Cross		Sp	Special
Gen	General		Spt	Support
Ger	German		Sqn	Squadron
			WN	*Wiederstandsnest*

How to use this Guide

This book is designed as a simple 'Pocket Guide' that will guide the visitor around the salient parts of the D-Day beaches and their memorials, cemeteries and museums.

What to do First

If you are unfamiliar with the background to the D-Day Landings then it is best first to **read** the short section '**Before D-Day**' and the subsequent pieces about the planning of the invasion and the German preparations to confront it.

If you just want to 'Tour the Beaches'

This book covers the landings that were made on the 6th June 1944 by the Allies from the sea and from the air onto and behind the five beaches named UTAH, OMAHA, GOLD, JUNO and SWORD.

Each beach is treated separately with its own section. First, at the head of each section, there is a short introduction explaining what happened on that beach on D-Day and then **a suggested battlefield tour with a clear start point** for each beach is laid out with timings, distances and background information on the battle sites, museums, memorials and cemeteries that make up the tour. There is a **map of each itinerary route**.

Thus, if you want to tour a beach area and get an overall view of what happened there, then go to the start point and take the tour for the beach that interests you. We give itemised timings so that you can plan your day.

If you wish to visit a Specific Place

If you just wish to go straight to a museum or a particular memorial then you should be able to find that in the index. We give key decimal latitude and longitude references which can be used on Google Earth or Microsoft Autoroute and many hand-held GPS devices, so that you can pin-point your objective and go directly to it. Do bear in mind, however, that there are slight variations in co-ordinates from system to system. If you wish to visit a particular grave then check the location with the Commonwealth War Graves Commission/American Battle Monuments Commission (see the **Allied and German Wargraves and Commemorative Associations** section).

Mark Up a Map

Whatever your planned visit is, it will be greatly enhanced if by using this book you mark up a suitable map with what you want to see, where you want to go and where you are staying before you leave home. We recommend our *Major & Mrs Holt's Battle Map of the Normandy D-Day Landing Beaches*; also Blay Foldex Normandie No. 103. In the **Tourist Information** section we give some advice on how to find the accommodation that suits your needs.

Before D-Day
Some Background History

World War Two Begins

At dawn on Friday 1 September 1939, nearly fifty German divisions, including six Panzer divisions, supported by over fifteen hundred aircraft, invaded Poland. It was the *Blitzkrieg* – the 'Lightning War'. The British mobilised and the French declared martial law.

On 5 October the last Polish troops surrendered near Warsaw and Poland was divided up between Russia, who on 17 September had also invaded Poland, and Germany. Then the invaders stopped.

The Phoney War

President Roosevelt sent emissaries from America to investigate the possibility of a negotiated settlement. The BEF went to France as a precaution against further invasion and the European nations eyed each other across the Franco-Belgian borders and prepared for war. Eight months later, after the period known as the Phoney War, or the *Sitzkrieg*, the Germans struck again.

Dunkirk

On Friday 10 May 1940 seventy seven German divisions invaded Belgium, Holland and Luxembourg. Once again the speed of the German offensive confused the defending forces and the BEF, which had been strung along the Belgian border, withdrew in some confusion to the Channel coast around Dunkirk. There between 26 May and 4 June over a quarter of a million British soldiers were evacuated. In England Winston Churchill became Prime Minister. On 22 June in Marshal Foch's old railway carriage near Compiègne, used for the German surrender in 1918, the French gave in and signed an armistice.

On 23 June Adolf Hitler toured Paris and the Germans considered how they could invade Britain.

The Battle of Britain

Hitler's plan for the invasion was called 'Operation SEALION' and he specified that before it could begin the "English Air Force must be eliminated". That task fell to the *Luftwaffe* under Reichsmarschall Hermann Goering who had over three thousand combat aircraft at his disposal.

On 13 August 1940, what the Germans called 'Eagle Day', the *Luftwaffe* offensive began and by 5 September the outnumbered RAF was on the point of collapse. Then, in retaliation for a bombing raid on Berlin, Hitler changed his plans and ordered an all-out offensive on London. The pressure on the RAF eased and, as it became clear that Britain could not be defeated quickly, Operation SEALION was cancelled. It was 17 September 1940.

The Blitz

But the bombing of London and other industrial cities by night that became known as 'The Blitz' continued until May 1941 by which time almost 40,000 civilians were killed and 46,100 were injured. In June Hitler invaded Russia and the pressure on Britain eased. Churchill now began to look across the Channel and he spoke to his Combined Operations Staff about an invasion going in the opposite direction to SEALION.

America Joins In

On 7 December 1941 Japanese aircraft attacked the American naval base at Pearl Harbour and on 11 December America declared war on Germany. At Christmas Prime Minister Winston Churchill and President Roosevelt met in Washington to plan Allied strategy. They agreed that there would have to be an invasion of Europe. **It would eventually be called OVERLORD and it would land in Normandy on a day called D-Day.**

The Planning for D-Day

The Commanders

In 1941, as it became clear to Hitler that Britain was not going to be defeated easily, he ordered a defensive wall to be built along the coastline from Norway to Spain with a planned 15,000 strongpoints. Known as the 'Atlantic Wall' it protected Hitler's 'Fortress Europe' and it was that wall that would have to be breached if the Allies planned invasion of Europe was to have any chance of success.

In Quebec in August 1943 Churchill and Roosevelt agreed upon a date for the invasion – it was 1 May 1944 and its code-name was OVERLORD. A month later General Eisenhower was appointed Supreme Commander and General Montgomery became the effective Ground Force Commander of the invasion forces.

The Deception Plan

It was clearly important that the Germans should not know where or when the invasion would take place. An elaborate plan named FORTITUDE was established for that purpose. The key to the plan was that the Germans should think **that the invasion would be in the area of Calais and not in Normandy**. Calais was after all a logical place to land as it was at the end of the shortest sea crossing from Britain.

Many ruses were used to persuade the Germans about the Calais landing including flying more air sorties in that area than in Normandy, intensive radio traffic around Dover suggesting that large forces were being assembled, the use of dummy tanks and the parading of General Patton (considered by the Germans to be the Allies' best field General) in the south-east and in command of an imaginary army.

A critical period for an assault landing comes just after the troops are ashore when the whole apparatus of supply has to be rewound in order to maintain and to re-inforce the formations already in position. Therefore it was vital that after the landings the Germans should then believe that Normandy was just a diversion and that the real landings would be around Calais. That way the main body of their troops would be kept around Calais in anticipation and not moved to Normandy.

FORTITUDE worked.

The Assault Plan

Troops making a sea landing are most vulnerable to attacks from their flanks. It was therefore decided that the beach assaults would have airborne landings at each end, effectively to seal off the beaches from German counter-attacks from the flanks.

Five beaches were selected. Two for the Americans in the west, UTAH and OMAHA, chosen so that re-supply for them could come straight across the Atlantic, and three in the east, GOLD, JUNO and SWORD, for the British and the Canadians.

In between the beaches, where there were gaps these would be tackled by Special Forces of US Rangers and British Commandos.

Five first assault divisions would land by sea, one per beach. Two American airborne divisions would seal the American beaches and one British airborne division would close off the British beaches. That was the plan.

Bad Weather – "OK. We'll go!"

There were two changes to the date for D-Day. On 8 May 1944, the 1943 date of May 1944 was changed to 5 June. The only other suitable days that month (because of the state of the tides) were the 6th or 7th. As the month of June opened the weather in the Channel became so bad that Eisenhower decided to postpone the invasion for at least 24 hours, the invasion fleet being told around 0400 on the 4th. Many of the 4,000 ships were already at sea and some had to turn around. At 0415 hours on 5 June Eisenhower sought the opinions of his fellow Commanders. Should he postpone again? The troops at sea were getting sea-sick and worst of all the Germans might find out what was going on. In response to Eisenhower's question about the weather he was told that there might be a brief lull in the next 48 hours. Knowing that with any more delay his army might not be fit to fight and that, even worse, the Germans might find out what was going on, at 0415 on 5 June Eisenhower said,

'OK. We'll go'.

The Germans and the Atlantic Wall

The Defences

The first elements of what was to become the Atlantic Wall were concrete naval gun emplacements sited along the Pas de Calais coast line in support of the proposed German invasion of Britain. After the invasion was called off the 70 or so positions already completed were incorporated into the plans for the 15,000 strong points to be built by the Todt Organisation along the whole coastline from Norway to Spain.

'The Führer at the Atlantic Wall'.

In February 1944 **Field Marshal Rommel** took over command of Army Group B, part of Army Group West commanded by Field Marshal von Rundstedt, and began an inspection of the Wall's defences. He found that they were far from complete and began an immediate and energetic programme to construct defensive works on the beaches.

Between December 1943 and May 1944 Rommel toured furiously, looking in particular at the Pas de Calais area. During April and May he concentrated upon Normandy, overseeing the placing of thousands of mines (one calculation of the total number of mines in the Atlantic Wall puts the figure at over 6 million), the construction of concrete and metal structures designed to stop landing craft on the beaches, such as 'Czech hedgehogs' (large three-dimensional six-pointed stars made by welding or bolting three pieces of angle-iron together), large wooden stakes with mines or shells attached to them, concrete tetrahedrons for anti-tank defence and a variety of other underwater obstacles designed to delay an invading force long enough for it to come under direct fire from the defenders. Hitler had had an inspiration that the invasion would come in Normandy and in addition to Rommel's efforts on the beaches the 91st Division was sent to Normandy with the 6th Parachute Regiment under command. Their specific task was that of defences against airborne landings.

Now it was a matter of who controlled the Panzers.

The Panzers and Command and Control

The big debate amongst the German leaders was how the panzer divisions should be used against an invasion. Although everyone believed that the key to the defeat of an Allied invasion lay with the armoured divisions, some, like Rommel, favoured holding the armour close behind the beaches so that an immediate counter-attack could be made. Others, like General Guderian, believed that the tanks should be held further back until the actual landing beaches were clearly identified, arguing that if the first policy were followed, and they guessed wrongly where the invasion would come, then disaster would follow. Both of them, however, believed that the invasion had to be stopped on the beaches but the Commander in Chief, von Rundstedt, thought that the invasion could not be stopped there and that the panzers should be held some way back until a massive and decisive counter-attack could be launched.

The situation was made even more complex by Hitler. Although he favoured Rommel's view that the first 48 hours after the landings would be critical, he only gave him direct control of three of the nine Panzer divisions. In theory the remaining six came under the command of von Rundstedt but even those could not be released without Hitler's authority.

Poor von Rundstedt had even more command challenges because he had no operational authority over the *Luftwaffe* or the Navy and so formations in Army Group B could, and did, receive orders from three different headquarters – Rommel's, von Rundstedt's and Hitler's.

On D-Day 6 June 1944

When he was appointed Rommel had split his command into two. He put his Seventh Army in the area west of the River Orne - that is exactly in the area east to west that covered Pegasus Bridge - SWORD Beach - JUNO Beach - GOLD Beach - OMAHA Beach - UTAH Beach - Cherbourg. Pretty well spot on. But his three Panzer divisions had to cover his entire Pas de Calais command. One was west of Paris and another was near Amiens. He had only one division available in the Normandy area - the 21st - and that was behind Caen and the British beaches.

On 3 June Rommel met von Rundstedt to discuss a planned visit to see Hitler during 5-8 June when he intended to ask for two more armoured divisions to be transferred to Normandy and at 0600 hours on the 4th of June, in the same bad weather that was troubling Eisenhower, Rommel left for Germany. He was going home for his wife's birthday. Surely the weather was too bad for an invasion.

Thus on the 6th June when the Allies landed in Normandy **Rommel was not there**.

Oddly he had been absent for one other important battle on the day that it had started - El Alamein. He lost that too.

Two Very Curious Things

In 1812 the Prussian military philosopher Carl von Clausewitz wrote a paper which led to the formulation of twelve principles of war that he believed were essential to success. One of them was 'Surprise'.

Clearly the **Deception Plan** which was designed to fool the Germans into thinking that the invasion would come across the shortest sea route towards Calais and not towards Normandy was how the Allies were going to achieve 'Surprise'. But two very curious things happened before D-Day that must have given them great concern that the secret had been leaked. The curious things were: -

ONE: On 2 May 1944, barely a month before D-Day, the answer to a clue in the ***Daily Telegraph* crossword** was "**Utah**". Then on the 22nd of May the answer to a clue in the crossword was "**Omaha**". On the 27th of May an answer was "**Overlord**". Then on the 30th an answer was "**Mulberry**" (the codeword for the floating harbours that were to be towed across the Channel). Finally, on 1 June an answer was "**Neptune**" (this was the Naval codeword for the invasion). Startled by the public appearance of so many secret invasion codewords two MI5 men visited the compiler, Leonard Dawe, the Headmaster of Strand School in

MAY 27, 194[

OLD BILL: BY BRUCE BAIRNSFATHER
"If yer asks me, mate, that's where Eisenhower's goin'
to land, right there !"

That's where
Eisenhower's goin' to land.'

Effingham, but apparently found no evidence of espionage. One explanation was given many years later by a former pupil of Dawe's who said that the Headmaster allowed boys to help him with the crossword and that he, the boy, had learned the words from Canadian and American soldiers camped near the school. What do you think?

TWO: The Deception Plan was designed to mislead the Germans into both when and where the invasion would take place. 'When' was difficult to conceal. Indeed on 18 May German radio broadcast that, 'The invasion will come any day now'. So they were expecting it. But they were not certain 'where' it would be. Yet on 27 May, the day that the *Telegraph* crossword contained the word "Overlord", the magazine John Bull published their 'Old Bill' cartoon by the famous First World War cartoonist Captain Bruce Bairnsfather. Old Bill is pointing to a map of Europe drawn on the side of a cow and is saying to his companion, "If yer asks me mate, that's where Eisenhower's going to land, right there!" He is pointing to the middle of the Normandy Landing Beaches. Very curious.

Some D-Day Statistics

The following tables are an amalgam from German, American and British sources and do not claim any absolute accuracy. They are designed only to give a comparative indication of factors that, relative to one another, help to put what happened into perspective.

ALLIED & GERMAN AIR & SEA STRENGTHS EFFECTIVE IN THE INVASION

D-Day *only*	Allied	German
Small ships and landing craft	4,270	3
Warships	600	NIL
Available Bombers	2,200	70
Available Fighters	5,000	90

AMERICAN LANDINGS AND CASUALTIES

D-Day *only*	82nd AB*	101st AB*	UTAH	OMAHA
Total landed	7,000	6,600	23,250	34,250
Total casualties	1,240	1,260	210	3,880

BRITISH AND CANADIAN LANDINGS AND CASUALTIES

D-Day *only*	GOLD	JUNO	SWORD	6AB*
Total landed	25,000	21,500	29,000	6,000
Total casualties	413	925	630	1,200

Note: casualties include killed, wounded and missing.
* Airborne Brigades

Latitude and Longitude References

References are given in decimal degrees compatible with Google Earth. North and East are positive. There may be small discrepancies if these figures are used with Microsoft Autoroute

ITINERARY ONE
US AIRBORNE OPERATIONS & UTAH BEACH

The American air and sea landings north of Carentan on the Cotentin Peninsula are so interdependent that the memorials, drop zones and beaches can be seen on one comprehensive Itinerary and therefore the background information for the 4th Division landing on UTAH, and the 82nd and 101st Divisions' airborne landings, precedes the tour.

THE AMERICAN AIRBORNE OPERATIONS

Drop Time:	0130 hours
Divisional Commanders	82nd: Major General Matthew B. Ridgway
	101st: Major General Maxwell Taylor
German Defenders:	91st Division
	709th Division
	6th Parachute Regiment
91st Division Commander:	Lieutenant General Wilhem Falley
709th Division Commander:	Lieutenant General Karl W. von Schlieben
6th Parachute Regiment Commander:	Major Friedrich-August von der Heydte

The Plan - The American Airborne Operations

The American airborne assault on D-Day was in its own right the largest ever to have been attempted. The two divisions, the 82nd 'All American' and the 101st 'Screaming Eagles', comprised six parachute infantry regiments (PIR), a total of over 13,000 men, including attached arms and services. The parachute assault alone needed 822 transport planes.

The broad plan was that the parachute divisions would secure exits from UTAH beach, gain control of the crossings over the rivers Merderet and Douve, prevent German counter movements along the N13 from Carentan or Valognes, and gain and secure landing grounds for reinforcement by glider at dawn and dusk. Ahead of the main bodies of the parachute troops pathfinders were to jump to mark the drop zones.

In particular the **82nd Division**, landing slightly north and to the west of the 101st, charged its 505th Regiment with taking the town of Ste Mère Eglise the 507th was to capture remaining bridges over the Merderet River and the 508th was to establish a defensive line west of the river in anticipation of counter-attacks

The **101st Division** had been created in August 1942 from the 82nd and was commanded by General Maxwell D. Taylor. Three drop zones were allocated to the paratroop forces with the tasks of securing the four exits from the beach that the seaborne force would need, and of taking and protecting the landing zone which was to be used by the division's gliders. Following these tasks the division was to seize the town of Carentan. Thus, if all went well, exits would be secured for the invasion forces arriving on UTAH beach and the flanks of the invasion force would be protected by the airborne forces.

On 5 June the **Supreme Commander** said to his British driver, Kay Summersby, 'I hope to God I know what I'm doing', and that evening they drove to Newbury where the General visited four airfields. He talked to General Maxwell Taylor and men of the 101st

Airborne Division, going from group to group, shaking hands and talking briefly to each man. 'It's very hard really to look a soldier in the eye,' he told Kay, 'when you fear that you are sending him to his death'.

What Happened on D-Day - The American Airborne Operations

The thick cloud and bad weather made it difficult to navigate and some of the pathfinders missed the drop zones and set up their homing beacons in the wrong places. Enemy flak caused the relatively inexperienced troop carrier pilots to take avoiding action. They therefore weaved and flew higher and faster than they should have done so that when the paratroopers jumped they were not only too high and moving too quickly, but they were probably also in the wrong place.

The **82nd Airborne Division**, dropping west of Ste Mère Eglise and astride the River Merderet, was more fortunate than the 101st. The 505th PIR, the first 82nd regiment to jump, landed pretty well on its drop zone, Zone 'O', and within three hours had taken Ste Mère Eglise thus controlling any movement by the Germans from Valognes down the N13. The 507th and 508th, were scattered west of the River Merderet which resembled less of a river and more of a broad ribbon of swamp.

The **101st Airborne Division** was distributed over an area of almost 400 square miles. By dawn only 1,100 men of the division's 6,600 had reached their reporting points and only a further 1,400 assembled by the end of the day. The countryside added to their confusion. Small fields bordered with strong hedges were typical. They all looked the same. It was difficult to know which way to go. Yet by 0600, 4½ hours after the main landing, the division had secured the western ends of the Exit causeways leading from UTAH. Without those Exits the 4th Division could not get off the beach because the ground around them was flooded and marshy. Thus, before the infantry had arrived, the 'Screaming Eagles' had virtually guaranteed the success of the UTAH landing.

UTAH BEACH LANDINGS

Assault time:	0630 hours
Leading Formations:	8th Regimental Combat Team of the US 4th Infantry Division
US 4th Division Commander:	Major General Raymond O. Barton
Bombarding Force A:	Battleship: USS *Nevada*
	Monitor: HMS *Erebus*
	Cruisers: USS *Tuscaloosa* (flagship)
	USS *Quincy*
	HMS *Hawkins*
	HMS *Enterprise*
	HMS *Black Prince*
	Gunboat: HNMS *Soemba* (Dutch)
	Eight destroyers
German Defenders:	709th Infantry Division and elements of 352nd Infantry Division
709th Division Commander:	Lieutenant General Karl W. von Schlieben
352nd Division Commander:	Lieutenant General Dietrich Kraiss

The Plan - UTAH Beach Landings

The plan was that before the landings, high-altitude heavy bombers followed by lower altitude medium bombers were scheduled to soften up the Atlantic Wall. Then, as the troops headed for the beaches, Allied warships were to shoot them in, keeping the defenders' heads down so that the assault troops could establish a bridgehead ashore.

General Barton, commanding the 4th Division, planned to land in a column two battalions wide with a frontage of just over 2,000 yards. Leading the assault was the 8th Infantry Regiment with attached to it the 3rd Battalion of the 22nd Infantry Regiment. The regiment's first task was to open the route inland by getting to the high ground in the area of Ste Marie du Mont (Exit 2, D913-les Forges, the D70 road) and then to push on to make contact with the 82nd Airborne Division to their north in the direction of Ste Mère Eglise. Ultimately the division was charged with driving on to take the port of Cherbourg.

What Happened on D-Day - UTAH Beach Landings

The weather was not good. Waves of five to six feet and winds of fifteen knots or more in mid-Channel made life uncomfortable for the men on the ships. The skies were overcast and the heavy bombers, who were to bomb the Atlantic Wall, could not see their targets and had to bomb by instruments alone. This fact, coupled with the 8th Air Force decision that there should be a delay of several seconds in releasing the bombs to avoid dropping any on the assault craft, meant that most of their 13,000 bombs fell too far inland. Sixty-seven of the 360 bombers of IX Bomber Command sent to UTAH failed to release their bombs at all because of poor visibility.

The medium bombers at a lower altitude fared better, but a third of their payload fell into the sea and many of their selected targets were not found. Thus the pre-landing aerial bombardment did little towards overcoming the coastal defences.

At about 0300 hours, some thirteen miles out to sea, the 4th Division began unloading from their transport ships into their LCVPs (Landing Craft, Vehicle & Personnel). It was a 3½-hour journey to the beach and before that began many men, overloaded with heavy equipment, fell or jumped from the rigging on the sides of the transports into their assault craft, breaking their legs on impact. Others, as the boats rose and fell in the choppy sea, missed the LCVPs altogether and fell into the water.

As the craft, each with about thirty men on board, headed for the shore, many soldiers were violently sea-sick. Yet they had much to be grateful for. The sea crossing had been unopposed and as the craft neared the shore the expected hail of German fire did not materialise.

At 0550 hours the heavy Allied naval bombardment began, concentrating upon locations where major German gun batteries were known to exist. Then, closer in, the cruisers opened fire upon coastal defences such as pill boxes and machine-gun posts. Finally, just before the LCVPs touched shore, the 'drenching fire' began. This was a torrent of high explosive fire by shallow draft vessels close in to shore, such as destroyers and LCVGs (Landing Craft, Vehicle & Gun). Then as the troops prepared to land, the fire lifted to the first vegetation line. It was the naval equivalent of the army's creeping barrage.

The LCVPs of the two assault battalions of the **8th Infantry Regiment** hit the sand on time. It was 0630 hours. The ramps went down and out came the GIs, relieved to be ashore but with a hundred yards of open beach to cross before reaching the shelter of the dunes and a low concrete wall on their seaward side. There was no opposition as they crossed the sand, but Brigadier General Theodore Roosevelt, the assistant divisional commander who accompanied the first wave, quickly realised that the Division had landed in the wrong place - 2,000 yards south of where they should have been.

Roosevelt decided that the mistake could not be corrected and cane in hand he strode up and down, exhorting men to get up and off the beach and to move inland. It was a wise decision and one which won him the Medal of Honour. The intended landing place was far more heavily defended than the spot where they had actually landed and though German artillery and small arms fire did sporadically harass the 4th Division as they poured ashore, casualties were very light.

It is unwise to be dogmatic about casualty figures since they are frequently manipulated for propaganda purposes by both sides in a conflict. However, by the end of the day, best estimates suggest that some 23,250 troops had come ashore and only 210 were killed, wounded or missing, less than one-third of those who died in the rehearsal on Slapton Sands.

THE BATTLEFIELD TOUR

THE TOUR STARTS AT STE MERE EGLISE
Planned duration without refreshment stops or extra visits: 3 hours 30 minutes.
Total distance: 16 miles.
The approach from the N13 is the same whether coming from direction Caen or Cherbourg. After taking the Ste Mère exit follow the D67 signed to the town.

* Ste Mère Eglise/0 miles/60 minutes/RWC
The D67 leads to a large sign on the left which proclaims '6 Juin 1944. D.Day. 505th Airborne. H Minus. General J.M. Gavin' and a crest. Before the board is a plaque which summarises the story of the 505th's action on D-Day. Behind it are 5 fir trees. Behind is the ** **Hotel-Restaurant le Sainte-Mère** (Logis de France). 41 rooms. Tel: +(0)2 33 21 00 30. Email: hotel-le-ste-mere@wanadoo.fr
Follow the road into the town along Rue du Général de Gaulle. On reaching the main square, Place 6 Juin, turn right. On the right is the

TOURIST OFFICE. Tel: +(0)2 33 21 00 33 E-mail: ot.stemereeglise@wanadoo.fr. This has reasonable opening hours and helpful staff.
On places of historical interest around the town are numbered **Information Panels**.
On the wall of the house before the Tourist Office is a **Plaque to Clifford A. Maughan**, who parachuted here.
Continue along Rue du Général Eisenhower and park in front of the church.
The sights in Ste Mère Eglise are best visited by walking. There is a variety of restaurants, snack bars and souvenir/book shops in the town. The local speciality is the

cheese *Petite Sainte Mère Eglise.*

Ste Mère owes much of its fame to an American called John Steele. Steele was a paratrooper of the 505th PIR of the 82nd Airborne Division and shortly after 0130 hours on the morning of 6 June he, and some thirteen thousand other airborne soldiers, jumped out of over 880 transport planes flying over Normandy. Steele fell onto the church steeple in Ste Mère Eglise, slid down it and then with his parachute caught on a flying buttress hung there for all to see. His story was told in the film, *The Longest Day.* After two hours John Steele was cut down and taken prisoner, probably the last prisoner taken before active resistance in the town ceased at 0430 hours. The town had been liberated, the first town in France to be so.

The task of taking the town had been that of the 3rd Battalion of the 505th PIR commanded by Lieutenant-Colonel Edward C. Krause who ordered his own men to enter Ste Mère Eglise by stealth, using knives and bayonets and, where necessary, grenades. The tactic worked. The Germans were taken by surprise. At 0930 hours the enemy counter-attacked from the south with two companies of infantry and some armour. Most of the 2nd Battalion under Lieutenant-Colonel Benjamin H. Vandervoort, which had established a defence line north of the town, moved back to help. The colonel broke an ankle in the drop but, using a stick as support, continued to command his battalion. The Germans then launched a simultaneous attack from the north onto the remnants of the 2nd Battalion which numbered forty-two men. When the attack and counter-attack sequence finally ended, some eight hours later, only sixteen of the forty-two men had survived. Both colonels were awarded the DSC for their conduct during the capture of Ste Mère Eglise, the medals being pinned on them in July by General Bradley himself. General Gavin was awarded the DSC at the same ceremony.

Start your **walking tour** *at the Museum, opposite the church on Rue du Général Eisenhower.*

• US Airborne Museum/Douglas C47/Commemorative Plaques/WC/Lat & Long: 49.40840 -1.31549

Outside the Museum is a **NTL Totem**. Begun on 6 June 1961 when General James Gavin laid the foundation stone, and housed in a parachute-shaped building, the Museum was designed by architect, François Carpentier, who had designed the successful museum at Arromanches.

There is an audio-visual show in 4 languages, touch screen information on the Battle of Normandy and films depicting the paratroopers' equipment and the C47. Veterans are asked to sign the Book of Honour. The most important addition has been that of the **C47 aircraft** *Argonia*, in a hangar shaped like a delta parachute, beside the museum. After its chequered career, including taking part in Operation MARKET GARDEN and working as a civilian aircraft, the Douglas C47 returned to Normandy, lovingly restored by Yves Tariel, President of the Parachutists' League of Friendship and his associates. It was unveiled in its custom-built museum here in June 1983.

In the garden is a Sherman tank. In June 1994 a **Marker to the 505th Parachute**

ITINERARY ONE
US AIRBORNE OPERATIONS / UTAH BEACH

Cherbourg
21 miles

E46 - N13

Exit 3   D67

UTAH Beach
Museum

UTAH BEACH

START   Ste-Mère-Eglise

D67

D14

Exit 2

▲ Iron Mike

▲ Écoquenéauville

D913

Exit 1

D70

▲ Chef-du-Pont

Ste-Marie-du-Mont ●

Douve

▲ Hiesville

Vierville ▲

▲ Angoville-au-Plain

D913

N

St Côme-du-Mont ▲
FINISH

Douve

Bayeux
27 miles

Itinerary 1   16 miles

0   1   2   3 miles

D913

E46 - N13

Carentan ●

Infantry Regiment was unveiled in the grounds and on a tree is a **Plaque to Private William H. Tucker** who landed in it on 6 June 1944. Tucker later became Vice-President of one of America's largest railways.

Open: daily 1 Feb-30 Nov from 1000-1230 and 1400-1800, from June -September from 0930-1900, from November-March weekends, bank and school holidays 1000-1230 and 1400-1730. Tel: +(0)2 33 41 41 35. e-mail: musee.airborne@wanadoo.fr

Entrance fee payable. Reductions for children, senior citizens and groups.

Beside the Museum is **Le Normandy Bar & Pizzeria**, Tel: +(0)2 33 21 25 25. Closed 15 Nov-10 Feb, then a house which was called *La Haule* in 1944, at whose entrance is a sign with a crest. It was to here on D-Day that the residents of Ste Mère carried buckets of water from the pump. The small cul de sac beside it is named after **Robert (Bob)**

Murphy, who landed there on 6 June. He survived the war and was a frequent visitor to Ste Mère.

Walk over to the Church.

During summer months an effigy of John Steele usually hangs from the church tower. Steele died in Kentucky in May 1969 and there is an ** **hotel/restaurant named 'The John Steele'** around the corner from the Place du 6 juin along rue du Cap-de-Laine. 7 rooms. Closed: Jan/Feb and 2 weeks in Nov. Tel: +(0)2 33 4141 16. E-mail: philippe.buquetz2@wanadoo.fr

Effigy of John Steele on Ste Mère Eglise Church.

• Stained Glass Windows, Church

There are two fine stained glass windows commemorating the US paratroopers. Over the portal is the predominantly blue window, designed by Paul Renaud, son of the 1944 mayor. It shows the Virgin Mary surrounded by paratroopers. On the 25th anniversary of the drop, in 1969, the veterans of the 82nd Airborne donated another stained glass window, which was dedicated on 4 June 1972. It shows St Michael, patron saint of the parachutists, and incorporates the Cross of Lorraine and various military insignia. Traces of machine-gun bullet marks can still be seen near the pulpit.

On leaving the church, walk left to

• *Pump.*
It was from here on the evening of 5 June that the line of villagers passed buckets of water to the house set on fire during the pre-invasion bombing.

At the opposite side of the square are:

• *Comité du Débarquement Monument and Alexandre Renaud Memorial*
The *Comité du Débarquement Monument Signal* is one of ten set up to commemorate the landings/liberation. Alexandre Renaud, mayor at the time of the Liberation, died in 1966. Monsieur Renaud was a distinguished author of books and novels about World War I (in which he was an officer), and wrote the most vivid and accurate contemporary account of the June 1944 drop: *Ste Mère Eglise: First American Bridgehead in France.*

Turn left along Rue Général de Gaulle back in the direction you drove into the town and turn first right. Continue almost to the end of the road to No 8 on the left.

• *Plaque, Rue de la Cayenne*
Erected on the house where four parachutists of the 505th were killed on 6 June 1944: '**Sgt Stanley Smith, Pfc William C. Walter, Pvt Robert L. Herrin and Pvt Robert E. Holtzmann.**' The first three are buried in the American Cemetery at St Laurent.

Return to the square and walk down rue des Ecoles to the left at the corner of the square to No 21.

• *Plaque to Two Troopers,* Jack Leonard and Bill Laws of No 1 Coy 505 CP killed here on 6-7 June 1944. It was unveiled in 2005.
Return to the Square and walk up rue Cap du Laine to

• *Town Hall Memorials/Flag/Kilometer Zero*
Outside the town hall is the pink marker stone of Kilometer Zero. The Kilometer Zero marker stones were erected in 1946. They follow the path of General Leclerc's Free French 2nd Armoured Division 'from Chad to the Rhine'. Behind Kilometer Zero is the Memorial to the twenty-two civilians of Ste Mère Eglise who died in the battle of June 1944, and to the left and right are small plaques commemorating the liberation of the first town in France. To the right and rear of the marker stone is a stone erected in tribute to Generals Gavin and Ridgway and 'all the gallant liberators of the town'. Inside the town hall is the great Stars and Stripes, the first US flag to be raised in liberated France. In addition there is a painting by a German soldier portraying the parachute drop of 4/5 June.

Return to the Square. Follow signs to D17/Camping/College of St Exupéry along Rue du 505 Airborne. Pass the **Hotel du 6 Juin**, 8 rooms, Tel: + (0)2 33 21 07 18, *closed end Oct-Feb on the left and fork right. After some 300 metres on the right is*

• *US Cemetery Marker Number One*
The commemorative stone is one of three marking the first three US cemeteries. There were some 3,000 soldiers buried here. By 10 June there were eight battlefield cemeteries

in the American sectors, but later these were concentrated in five places - St Laurent, Blosville, Ste Mère Eglise, La Cambe and Orglandes. Then in March 1948 they were either re-interred into the one National Cemetery at St Laurent or sent home to America. The sports field behind the marker was where a set was built for making the film *The Longest Day* and actor Red Buttons played the part of John Steele on a recreated steeple.

*Return to the Square and your car. **Set your mileometer to 0.***

Drive out of Ste Mère Eglise by returning to Rue du Général de Gaulle. Turn left back in the direction that you came and continue on the D67, rue du Général de Gaulle, through Ecoqueneauville, to the crossroads with the D14. Continue on the D67 through Audoville-la-Hubert (this road was known as Exit 3) to the junction with the D421 Beach road. Turn right and continue to the Museum parking area.

• UTAH Beach Museum/US Memorials/8.5miles/45 minutes/RWC/Lat & Long: 49.40318 -1.19619

It is helpful to walk down to the beach and to consider the basic story of what happened here before going into the museum. The area had been visited by Rommel early in May in line with Hitler's premonition about Normandy being a likely invasion target. When Rommel was pleased with what he found he often gave a concertina or mouth-organ to one of the soldiers putting up obstacles, but when he came here he was not pleased.

He inspected the beach and the obstacles, and then demanded that Lieutenant Arthur Jahnke, in charge of blockhouse W5, take off his gloves and show his palms. Jahnke did so and, on seeing the weals and scratches on the young officer's hands, Rommel relented and told him that the blood he had spilled in putting up obstacles was as important as any he would spill in combat. Early on the morning of 6 June Jahnke was in W5, woken by the noise of aeroplanes and puzzled by the sound of gun fire coming from the direction of Ste Marie du Mont. He despatched a patrol to find out what was going on and to his surprise they returned in half an hour with seventeen American prisoners. The Americans told him nothing.

Then the air and naval bombardment began. Huge spouts of sand, pieces of concrete and clouds of dust filled the air. In little more than half an hour W5 was ineffective. Jahnke was wounded. As the noise lessened and the disorientated defenders looked out to sea they saw the approaching armada and, in the leading waves, floating tanks. The lieutenant tried to activate his own tanks, small wire-controlled tractors carrying explosives, called GOLIATHS, but they would not start

GOLIATHS being examined by US soldiers.

The Americans charged up the beach and rushed W5. Jahnke and his men surrendered. In 1987 Arthur Jahnke returned to W5 and shook hands with another veteran of that 6 June - an American of the 8th Infantry Regiment who had led the charge ashore.

Force U for UTAH had launched its thirty-two DD tanks only 2 miles from shore, instead of the planned 4 miles, because of the bad weather. It was a wise decision and twenty-eight tanks made it to the beaches providing direct fire support to the infantry and helping the assault engineers to deal with obstacles. The costly lesson of Dieppe had been learned. By midday UTAH Beach was clear and the 4th Division was on its way inland across the causeways to link up with the airborne forces.

By the end of the day the 4th Division had achieved almost all of its immediate objectives. Over the beach had come 23,000 men and 1,700 vehicles. The causeways were secure and the beachhead firm.

The Museum, offers a splendid account of the events that took place here on 6 June 1944 and immediately thereafter. Funded by the local Ste Marie du Mont council, the region and veterans, it was originally built into and around German Blockhouse W5 and now offers a panoramic view over the sea. It has landing craft, films using actuality footage (English sound available), diorama, scale models, photographs, ephemera and artefacts, many donated over the years by veterans. Postcards, books and maps are on sale. To the right of the desk in the entrance is a **Plaque to 238th Combat Engineers**.

Open: daily April, May 1000-1800. June-Sept 0930-1900. Oct 1000-1230 and 1400-1800. 1-15 Nov, Feb and March 1000-1200 and 1400-1730. 16 Nov-31 Dec, weekends and school holidays 1000-1200 and 1400-1730. Closed Jan. Entrance fee payable. Reductions for children. Tel: +(0)2 33 71 53 35. e-mail: musee.utahbeach@wanadoo.fr There are good parking, toilet facilities beside the museum.

Around and about the museum the following memorials and objects may be found within walking distance;

Outside the Museum is a **LEC Memorial** (qv).

'Thank God for the United States Navy!', said Maj-Gen Leonard Gerow, commander V Corps, to Lt Gen Omar Bradley on 6 June 1944 and finally, on 27 September 2008, a **US Navy Normandy Monument** was inaugurated on the highest point overlooking UTAH Beach on land donated by the French. It is approached up '**Voie Gen Dwight Eisenhower**, 1890-1969, Supreme Commander 6 June', as a **plaque** to the right at the top proclaims. The idea of the monument was that of Cristy and Ray Pfeiffer of Historic Tours. Ray told the Naval Order of the USA (NOUS - a fraternal society of America's sea-services and others) that there was no major D-Day US Navy Monument in Normandy. NOUS raised the required $500,000 and Stephen Spears sculpted the monument at his own expense. The NOUS, the Commune of Ste Marie du Mont and Historic Tours co-operated to co-ordinate the project. The inauguration ceremony was magnificent and extremely moving as the French Chief of Naval Staff presented the *Légion d'Honneur* to the three UTAH Beach veterans who had made the journey to France: **Capt Richard Zimmerman, CIC Officer USS Frankford, James Gaff, LCVP Coxswain and Chester Collins.**

Opposite is the **Café and bar *Le Roosevelt***, built adjoining a bunker which doubles as a most interesting little Museum .It serves snacks and simple meals and sells

The Museum, UTAH Beach, with Bunker.

US Navy Memorial, UTAH BEACH.

US Federal Monument
with, behind, 1st Special
Engr Bde Monument,
UTAH Beach.

postcards and souvenirs and is a great place to have a warming *café-calva* on a cold and blustery day on UTAH Beach.Tel: +(0)2 33 71 53 47. E-mail: info@le roosevelt.com **Closed:** Dec-mid Feb.

NTL Totem, Sherman Tank, Landing Craft, US Anti-aircraft Gun.

4th Division Memorial Obelisk.

Kilometer 00 - This marks the beginning of 4th Division's and Leclerc's 2nd Armoured Division's Liberty Highway which runs both into Holland and across France to the German border

Rowe Road Marker at exit from beach.

40th Anniversary commemorative plaque, naming King Baudouin of the Belgians, Queen Elisabeth II, King Olav V of Norway, Grand-Duke Jean of Luxembourg, Queen Beatrix of the Netherlands, President Reagan, Prime Minister Pierre Trudeau of Canada and President Francois Mitterand.

Bronze plaque, Voie General Eisenhower, 1890-1969

Bunker System A. This carries the 24ft-tall polished red Baveno granite memorial obelisk to the **American forces of VII Corps**, who landed here and liberated the Cotentin Peninsula between 6 June and 1 July 1944. It bears the words 'Erected by the United States of America in humble tribute to its sons who lost their lives in the liberation of these beaches. June 6, 1944'.

There is also a **Marker** to **90th Infantry Division**, the first follow-up division. It commemorates their dead from 6 June 1944 to 9 May 1945, and proudly carries the division's nickname, 'The Tough Hombres', and the fact that from UTAH Beach to Czechoslovakia the 90th Combat Team fought five campaigns in 300 days.

On top of the steps is a **Memorial** to the **1st Engineer Special Service Brigade** and a **light anti-aircraft gun**. On the low wall to the seaward side of the Engineer Memorial are fifty-eight markers pointing to ship locations, to where acts of heroism were performed (including Free French pilots), to ports and towns and even to Berlin.

Below, and part of, the bunker is a **memorial crypt** with an illuminated display including a **portrait of Major General Eugene Mead Caffey**, who was responsible for erecting the memorial. This is nor always open. As Colonel Caffey he commanded the Brigade in 1944 and dedicated the memorial on 11 November that year. In and on the walls of the crypt are plaques from or about:

> *Souvenir Français;* **Major General Eugene Mead Caffey; The Commander of the 1st US Engineer Special Brigade; The use of the blockhouse by the US engineers; The names of those Engineers who gave their lives; The actions of the airborne and seaborne forces on D-Day; Plaque to the US Coastguards.**

Some 250 metres to the east, down a small road to the left, **is a Memorial to the US Naval Reserve**.

[At this stage you may wish to visit the Mémorial de la Liberté Retrouvée Musée at Quinéville. Lat & Long: 49.51498 -1.28691

Go 9 miles westward along the D241 coast road.

En route you will pass some well-preserved **bunker** remains and a **Com Deb Sig**

Memorial group to Gen Leclerc's landings.
Continue to Quinéville, following signs to the Museum at the edge of the sea.
This fascinating Museum, partly housed in a bunker, specialises in life under the occupation with life-like street scenes; also a film *From Utah Beach to Cherbourg*. Well worth a visit. **Open:** daily 1 April-11 Nov 1000-1900. Tel: + (0)2 33 95 95 95. E-mail: memorial.quineville@wanadoo.fr Website: www.memorial-quineville.com Entrance fee payable.]
Leave UTAH BEACH Museum area on the D913 (this was Exit 2) signed to Ste Marie du Mont.

Exit 2

Exit, or causeway, 2 is typical of the four exits that were the only routes by which the seaborne invasion force would be able to get off the beach (there were three other possible routes but these were not felt to be suitable). The whole area had been flooded and nowadays it is difficult to imagine how it must have looked and how vital it was to secure the causeways, which were in effect pathways across a swamp. The task of controlling Exit 2 was that of 506th PIR, but their transport planes only managed to put ten loads out of eighty-four in the right place. However, Lieutenant-Colonel Strayer, who commanded the 2nd Battalion, and who had dropped four miles north of here, gathered elements of his battalion, plus some men of the 82nd Division who had dropped even further off target, and fought his way south. By 1330 he had Exit 2 under control. Along the roadside are markers naming part of the road after non-commissioned American soldiers. There are forty-three of them marked by seventy-six signs.
Continue to the Memorial on the left.

• UTAH Danish Memorial/9.5 miles/5 minutes

This Memorial, raised in 1984 and designed by Danish architect Svend Lindhardt, commemorates the 800 Danes who took part in the landings. The Danes, mostly serving on board ships, were those who had escaped from Denmark and were attached as individuals to British units.
Continue to Ste Marie du Mont.

• Ste Marie du Mont, Musée de l'Occupation, Musée de la Libération/11.7 miles/40 minutes/Lat & Long: 49.37863 -1.22551

The church here was probably the first thing that the Americans who dropped in this area recognised as the sky lightened. It enabled them to deduce where they were.

The drop had been in darkness and very badly scattered, and, as the men of the 'Screaming Eagles' landed among the hedgerows and small fields, or fell into the flood water, they suddenly felt alone. The noise of the aeroplanes and the crack of the flak explosions had gone. Now everything was unfamiliar and in the moonlight every shadow a threat. Each man had been given a small metal click-clack device which made a noise like a cricket and in a staccato avalanche of snapping noises men gradually came together.

Liberation Museum, Ste Marie du Mont.

Original German Murals, Occupation Museum, Ste Marie du Mont.

Dead Man's Corner Museum and the Paratrooper Militaria Emporium.

UTAH Danish Memorial, Exit 2.

General Maxwell Taylor, commanding the 101st Division, dropped just south of the village. As the divisional history puts it, 'The commander of 14,000 men found himself on a battlefield without a single one of those men within sight or hearing, any order he might have given would have been received only by a circle of curious Normandy cows.

The *Commune* of Ste Marie du Mont has placed a dozen or so signs around the village which describe the actions in the area. In the church are modern commemorative stained glass windows, replacements for those destroyed during the fighting, and opposite is the **Hotel /Restaurant 'Estaminet'** which provides a variety of menus. 4 rooms. Tel: +(0)2 33 71 57 01. Beside it is the **Crêperie Montoise**, Tel: +(0)2 71 90 28. Both are open every day June-Sept. The Estaminet closes Tues evening and all day Wed off season. The Crêperie is open Sat evening and Sun lunch May-June.

Round the square at No 36, the old Hospice Monvérand for four years home to the German 1st Coy, 919th Grenadiers HQ, is the small **Museum of the Occupation**. There are outstanding original German drawings from 1942 on the walls **Open:** 1 April-30 Sept every day 1000-1230 and 1330-1900, otherwise by appointment for groups. Entrance fee payable. Tel: +(0)2 33 71 57 14. E-mail: maxence.lepesant@hotmail.fr

Opposite, at 4 Place de l'Eglise, is the **Musée de la Libération** which describes the dramatic scenes of the night of 6 June with a fine collection of uniforms, weapons, vehicles (like the rare Weasel M29) and soldiers' personal items. Entry fee payable. **Open:** every day 1 April-11 November 1000-1200 and 1400-1800. Tel: +(0)2 33 71 25 62. E-mail: museedelaliberation@orange.fr

On the wall of the *Mairie* is a **Plaque** paying tribute to the soldiers of the **101st US AB** who liberated the village on June 1944

Continue through the village on the D913 along rue du Carentan through Vierville.
150 yards over and beyond the motorway bridge stop at the Museum on the right.

• Dead Man's Corner Museum, Paratrooper Militaria Emporium, St Côme du Mont/16 miles/30 minutes/ Lat & Long 49.32857N -1.26841W

The Museum's name dates from 7 June when in the American attack on Carentan the first tank to arrive at this crossroads was brought to a stop by the enemy and the Tank Commander was mortally wounded. His body hung outside the turret for several days.

In June 1944 the building had been requisitioned by the German 6th Parachute Regiment under Major von der Heydte and there is a remarkably lifelike depiction of his Command Room as one enters. Upstairs one moves from ship to tank to aircraft (don't forget to look up in the roof where a US Para is landing!). Audio-visual presentation. **The Paratrooper**, that adjoins the museum, is a veritable Aladdin's Cave for Militaria collectors with high quality souvenirs and artefacts for sale. Outside exhibits include a French Chenillette and a German 88mm gun.

Open: Every day other than Sundays from 15 Oct-30 May. **Closed:** 24, 25, 31 Dec and 1 Jan. Entrance fee payable. Tel: +(0)2 33 42 00 42. E-mail: Carentan.101@orange.fr Website: www. paratrooper.fr

The road that runs past the house is called Purple Heart Lane.

• End of Itinerary One

ITINERARY TWO
US RANGERS OPERATIONS POINTE DU HOC & OMAHA BEACH

'Bloody OMAHA' is how most Americans who know refer to the more easterly of the American landing beaches. OMAHA was the critical beach and on the 4 miles of sands below its 100ft high frowning cliffs the Allied invasion came perilously close to failure. Once again, as with the paratroopers, it was the spirit and determination of small groups of GIs that won through.

OMAHA BEACH LANDINGS

Assault Time:	0630 hours
Leading Formations:	116th IR (attached from 29th Division) and 16th IR of the 1st Infantry Division
US 1st Division Commander:	Major General Clarence R. Huebner
Bombarding Force C:	Battleships: USS *Texas* (flagship) USS *Arkansas* Cruisers: HMS *Glasgow* FFS *Montcalm* (French) FFS *Georges Leygues* (French) Eleven destroyers
German Defenders:	352nd Infantry Division and elements of 716th Coastal Defence Division
352nd Division Commander:	Lieutenant General Dietrich Kraiss

The Plan - OMAHA Beach Landings
General Huebner's plan was to attack on a two-regiment front with the 16th Regiment on the left and the 116th Regiment on the right.

It was a set-piece plan that had been prepared in great detail. The beach had been divided into eight sectors of different lengths beginning with DOG in the west and ending with FOX in the east.

What Happened on D-Day
The effect of the weather on Force O for OMAHA was far worse than on Force U for UTAH because the 1st Division did not have the benefit of shelter at sea from the Cotentin Peninsula. The troops were loaded into their assault craft some eleven miles offshore and in the dark with inevitable confusion. Then six thousand yards offshore twenty-nine DD (duplex drive) floating tanks were launched. Only two of these reached the beach.

As the leading waves of landing craft approached the shore they were off target, without their beach-clearing engineers, without supporting armour and short on artillery.

The men, crouched down in the bellies of the LCVPs, had been there for three hours. They were cramped, cold and sea-sick. Before they reached the shore, the enemy opened fire on them and what happened is graphically portrayed in Stephen Spielberg's film *Saving Private Ryan*. Nevertheless, despite all difficulties, by the end of D-Day the Americans were on the cliffs above the beach.

THE BATTLEFIELD TOUR

THE TOUR STARTS AT THE GERMAN CEMETERY AT LA CAMBE

* Planned duration without stops for refreshments or extra visits: 4 hours 45 minutes
* Total distance: 21 miles

Take the N13-E46 dual carriageway, continue to the La Cambe exit and follow signs to Cimetière Militaire Allemand on the D113. Set your mileometer to zero.

- *The German Cemetery/Exhibition/Peace Garden, La Cambe/0 miles/30 minutes/Lat & Long 49.34304N 1.02598W*

The Cemetery. The German People's Organisation for the care of War Graves (*Deutsche Kriegsgräberfürsorge*) established, and continues to care for, this and similar cemeteries. (See War Graves Organisations below).

To the left and right of the arched entrance are rooms which house the visitors' book, the cemetery registers, the names of the missing and war graves literature.

Inside the cemetery are small groups of black stone crosses. These are symbolic and do not mark graves. The graves are marked by flat stones engraved with the names of those below - often four or more together. Here there are 21,139 dead, including 296 in a mass grave under the grassed mound in the centre of the cemetery. The mound, or ossuary, is ringed at the bottom by stones carrying the names of the dead and surmounted by a huge black cross and two figures representing mourning parents.

The Exhibition/Information Centre and Peace Garden. The aim here is to show how war affected the individual and there are many moving displays of photographs and letters of soldiers (German and Allied) who died in Normandy. There is a computer with which visitors can look up the burial place/memorial of all the soldiers on both sides who are commemorated in Normandy. Tel +(0)2 31 22 70 76. E-mail: Lucien-tisserand@volksbund.de **Open:** Cemetery 0800-1900/Information Centre 0800-1200 and 1300-1900.

On the day of the inauguration a Peace Garden was started, which now stretches along the side of the road towards Bayeux. Each of its more than 1,000 trees is sponsored by an individual, an organisation or a municipal community. There is a **NTL Totem** beside the garden. On it are the words, 'With its melancholy rigour it is a graveyard for soldiers not all of whom had chosen either the cause or the fight.'

ITINERARY TWO
US RANGERS OPERATIONS / OMAHA BEACH

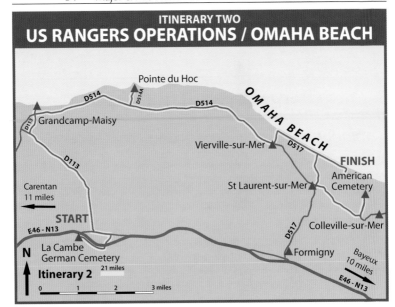

German Cemetery, la Cambe.

Return to the roundabout and follow signs to la Cambe and Grandcamp-Maisy on the D113/613 on a road with frequent twists and turns. Continue on the D113 to the small crossroads with Jucoville and les Vignets. Continue on the D113 into Grandcamp-Maisy and follow signs to the Port.

There are some fine sea food restaurants around the harbour, which become very popular on Sundays in the season, notably **La Marée**, 5 Quai Henri Chéron. Tel: +(0)2 31 21 41 00.

TOURIST OFFICE. 118 rue Aristide Briand. Tel: +(0)2 31 22 62 44. E-mail: grandcamp.tourisme@wanadoo.fr

Stop on the quay as near to the sea as possible. On the corner is

(Above) *Rangers' Museum, Grandcamp Maisy.*

(Left) *World Peace Statue, Grandcamp Maisy.*

(Below) *The Pointe du Hoc with the Rangers' Memorial on the cliff top.*

(Inset) *Rangers' Memorial.*

• *Monument to Heavy Group Bomber Command RAF/5.6 miles/10 minutes/RWC/Lat & Long: 49.38946 -1.04697*

The French squadrons, Groupe Guyenne and Groupe Tunisie, formed part of No 4 Group Bomber Command (Yorkshire Group), and were given the RAF numbers 346 and 347 respectively. On 5 June 1944 the targets for their Halifaxes were German gun emplacements just outside Grandcamp-Maisy, hence the Memorial which was unveiled on 8 June 1988

Walk some 400 yards along the seafront on the Quai Crampon, which has a No Entry sign. Stop at the Museum on the right.

• *Rangers Museum/Rangers & De Gaulle Memorials/30 minutes*

The Museum tells the story of the Rangers' heroic actions at Pointe du Hoc with a short film texts, photos, models, dioramas and personal effects

Open: 16 May-31 Oct 0930-1300 and 1430-1830 (closed Monday mornings). 15 Feb-15 May 1300-1800 (closed Mondays). Entrance fee payable. Tel: +(0)2 31 92 33 51. E-mail: GRANDCAMP-MAISY@ wanadoo.fr By the Museum is a **NTL Totem**.

Return to your car and turn left signed Centre Ville. Continue to the junction with the D514.

• *National Guard/Sergeant Peregory Memorial/Memorial Gardens/Statue of Peace/6.5 miles/5 minutes*

The monument and the memorial garden behind it were inaugurated on the 50th Anniversary. Sergeant Frank Peregory won the Medal of Honor for an action on 8 June when he captured 35 enemy soldiers. He is buried in the Normandy Cemetery. Beside the Memorial is a gigantic, 10m high, 12 ton, angel-like steel **Statue** representing **World Peace**. It was sculpted by Chinese artist Yao Yan of the Statue of World Peace Foundation.

Continue on the D514, direction Vierville sur Mer/Pointe du Hoc. At the roundabout turn to the left to Pointe du Hoc. Stop in the large parking area as close to the Visitor Centre as possible.

• *Pointe du Hoc/Ranger Memorial/Bunkers/Visitor's Centre/8.8 miles/30 minutes/WC/Lat & Long: 49.39492 -0.98928*

The Visitor's Building has a receptionist, WCs and parking area with a very long walk to the actual site then a signed walking route (suitable for wheelchairs) with 23 points at which there are bronze explanatory plaques. There is an explanatory **NTL Totem** at the entrance and an I**nformation Board**. Craters and bunkers remain with viewing platforms which give good views over the site and the landing beaches. In the reception building are two bronze **Plaques** commemorating the feat of the **Rangers. Open:** 1 April-31 Oct every day 1000-1300 and 1400-1800; 2 Nov-31 March Fri-Mon 0900-1300 and 1400-1700.   **Closed** 1 Nov, 25 Dec and 1 Jan. Tel: +(0)2 31 51 90 70.   E-mail: pointeduhoc@wanadoo.fr

The gun battery here was thought to be six 155mm, with a range of 25,000 yards and capable of firing on both UTAH and OMAHA. The area was bombed during May and June and then again during the night of the 5th. The potential threat was seen to be so great that Ranger Battalions were given the task of capturing the position directly after H-Hour.

The battery position is set upon cliffs that drop vertically some 100ft to a very small rocky beach. In addition to the main concrete emplacements, there were trenches and machine-gun posts behind and at the cliff's edge. The German garrison numbered about two hundred.

The position was out on a limb, some 4 miles from DOG Green, the nearest edge of the main OMAHA beach at Vierville. Between them was another prominent feature, Pointe de la Percée, which like Pointe du Hoc, jutted out into the sea. The assault force of three companies of 2nd Ranger Battalion was commanded by Lieutenant-Colonel James E. Rudder. He planned to land below the cliffs, climb them and then make a direct assault on the battery.

On D-Day the Rangers were late. The strong easterly tide had pulled them too far east, and in the morning the Rangers mistook Pointe de la Percée for Pointe du Hoc.

Walk along the James E. Rudder footpath to the Ranger Memorial at the edge of the cliff.

Over to the right the prominent feature jutting into the sea is Pointe de la Percée. Realising his mistake, the Colonel turned his small flotilla of seven British-crewed LCAs (three had already sunk in the heavy seas and the men were bailing out with their steel helmets in the ones which remained afloat), and moved in this direction, parallel to the shore and some 100 yards out. They landed some 500 yards away to your right and there Colonel Rudder established his HQ, featured in a well known photograph showing the spread-out American flag. Then, using ladders and daggers the Americans began to climb.

As they struggled to the top of the cliffs, they had direct and very effective fire support from the US destroyer *Satterlee* and the British destroyer *Talybont* and once on top, the Rangers, scattering small arms fire around them, worked quickly across the torn and smoking ground to the gun emplacements. When they got there they found that the guns had been removed.

Moving inland the Rangers found five of the guns in an area behind the roundabout and destroyed them. To this point, despite the difficulty of the assault, the Americans' casualties had been relatively light, probably thirty to forty, but later that day the Germans began a series of counter-attacks that nearly wiped out the small bridgehead. Aware of the isolation of the men at Pointe du Hoc, the US 116th Infantry Regiment, with the 5th Ranger Battalion which had landed with them at OMAHA four miles to your right (east), attempted to break through but were stopped 1,000 yards short. Not until 8 June were the 116th and the 5th able to join up with Point du Hoc. Before that, however, they had been bombed by Allied planes and fired on by their own side. Such is the fog of war. Their final casualties were 135 killed, wounded and missing out of a total of 225 that landed at Pointe du Hoc. This is a casualty rate of 60 per cent.

In 1954 James Rudder returned to Pointe du Hoc with his 14-year-old son Bud. His visit was covered by a feature in the 11 June 1954 issue of *Collier's* magazine, with a picture of father and son on the cover.

The memorial area is 30½ acres and the site was preserved by the *French Comité de la Pointe du Hoc*. The Ranger's granite 'dagger' Memorial sits on a German concrete OP bunker, with inscriptions in English and French. In the bunker below are **Plaques to Col Rudder and the 2nd Rangers**. The ground is still scarred with huge craters from the bombing or from the 14in guns of the USS *Texas*. On 6 June 1944 Pointe du Hoc must have been the nearest earthly equivalent to Hades.

Return to the D514 and follow the signs to Vierville/OMAHA Beach.

It was on OMAHA that the Americans suffered their most grievous losses - almost one-third as many again as the combined totals of the 82nd Airborne Division, the 101st Airborne Division and UTAH Beach, and more than the entire total of all British casualties for D-Day. As a result, OMAHA Beach has become a particular place of pilgrimage with a number of memorials and features to be seen.

Return to the roundabout and continue along the D514 towards Vierville Château.
On the left is

• MUSEE D.DAY OMAHA/13.3 miles/15 minutes

In an old hangar this contains many rare pieces of materiel – American, British, Canadian, French and German, including an Enigma machine, the collection of proprietor M Brissard. Outside is a 60-ton armoured cloche from a German coastal battery, dragons' teeth and a concrete German sentry box. There is a car park. **Open:** Varied times from 15 February - 15 November - basically in spring from 1000-1230 and 1300-1800, in summer from 0930-1930. Admission fee payable. Tel: +(0)2 31 21 71 80. Website: www.dday-omaha.net There is an **NTL Totem** by the entrance.

Continue. One hundred metres on the right is

Musée D.Day OMAHA, Vierville.

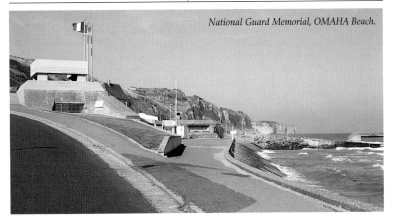

National Guard Memorial, OMAHA Beach.

• HQ 11th Port US Army, Vierville Château/13.4 miles/5 minutes

There is a **Plaque** on the right hand gatepost to commemorate the HQ.

Turn left down the D517.

On the left is a **5-span bridging section**, 507 A-B1, part of the floating bridge which formed part of the Omaha Beach artificial harbour.

Beyond and on the right are

• 5th Ranger Battalion Plaque/6th Engineer Special Brigade and 29th Infantry Div and J.R. Sainteny Memorials/13.7 miles/10 minutes

To the right is the **6th Engineers Special Brigade Memorial**. On D-Day the failure to neutralise the beach defences meant that the 6th Engineer Special Brigade, coming in with the second wave, was unable to get on with its job of blowing gaps in the obstacles. Of sixteen bulldozers only three were able to operate on the beach and by the end of the day casualties had reached 40%. Such was the heroism of the troops in tackling the obstacles that fifteen officers and men were awarded the Distinguished Service Cross.

The **Rangers' Plaque** is on the wall to the left. Colonel Rudder's force had consisted of the 2nd and 5th Ranger Battalions. Below it is the **29th (Blue and Grey) Division Memorial**. On the heights to the right is a German gun position. At the bottom is a **Memorial** naming the Square after French Resistance worker, **Jean Roger Sainteny**, codenamed 'DRAGON', 1907-1978.

Continue down the road to the sea. Stop in the car park beside the memorial at the bottom.

To the left is the **Hotel du Casino** run by M et Mme Clemencon. Tel: +(0)2 31 22 41 02. **Open:** April-11 November. Restaurant with splendid views over OMAHA, menus from simple and quick to gourmet. 2 star Logis de France. 12 rooms.

• National Guard Memorial/58th Armoured Field Artillery Memorial/Bunkers/13.8 miles/10 minutes/RWC/Lat & Long: 49.37924 -0.90281

OMAHA Beach and the 'Pals Battalion'

The general aspect of the memorial is that of a three-sided concrete box and a Plaque in English and in French thanks the people of Vierville for helping to build the Memorial and is dated June 1989. On opposite arms on the outside of the box are quotations from Winston Churchill and Charles de Gaulle.

Inside the arms of the Memorial the story of the National Guard is told in English and in French and the whole structure has been built upon blockhouse WN72. The Germans had built two *Wiederstandsnest* (WN) 'resistance points' to cover each of the five exits from the beach. On D-Day this position's two casemates, one with a 50mm weapon and the other with a 75mm gun, enfiladed the beach left and right. The position was overcome by a Sherman DD of 743 Tank Battalion shortly after mid-day. Where you are is effectively the western end of OMAHA Beach and it stretches away to the right in a concave arc for almost four miles. Nowhere less than 100ft high, cliffs stand guard over the seashore. You are standing at the entrance to the Vierville exit (draw), D1. (DOG 1). On the right hand side of the path down to the beach from the Memorial is another Memorial - to the **US 58th Armoured Field Artillery**, a unit equipped with 105 self-propelled guns, and beside it a **NTL**.

Below the cliffs is a mixture of dunes, scrub and waterpools leading down to the beach road on the sea-side of which is a wall marking the edge of the beach some six feet below. The beach is broad and flat and at low tide a good 100 yards separate the beach wall from the water's edge. Those 100 yards are clearly visible to anyone on the cliffs.

The 1st Division's landing plan was simple. The beach was divided into two main sectors, DOG where you are now, and EASY to the east (to the right). On DOG would land the 116th Infantry Regiment under command from the 29th Division and on EASY the 16th Infantry Regiment. Each regiment had attached to it supporting forces to help it in its task - two battalions of floating DD tanks to provide direct fire support against enemy fortified positions and two special brigades of engineers to clear beach obstacles. The combined forces were known as RCTs (Regimental Combat Teams), i.e. the 116th RCT and 16th RCT. It was planned that by the end of D-Day the 1st Division force would have a bridgehead 16 miles wide and 5 miles deep. In reality by nightfall on the day the bridgehead was barely the length of the beach and averaged less than 1 mile deep with most units still below the cliffs.

The leading company of the 116th Regiment was Company 'A'. It came ashore below where the National Guard Memorial stands and it was here right below you that the Americans suffered their worst casualties. It is this action that opens *Saving Private Ryan*.

One veteran remembered: -

Within 7 to 10 minutes after the ramps had dropped, Company A had become inert, leaderless and almost incapable of action. The Company was almost entirely bereft of Officers. All the officers were dead except Lieutenant Elijah

Nance who had been hit in the head as he left the boat, and then again in the body as he reached the sands. Lieutenant Edward Tidrick was hit in the throat as he jumped from the ramp into the water. He went on to the sands and flopped down 15ft from Pvt Leo J. Nash. He raised up to give Nash an order. Him bleeding from the throat and heard his words: 'ADVANCE WITH THE WIRE CUTTERS!' It was futile, Nash had no wire cutters. In giving the order, Tidrick himself a target for just an instant, Nash saw machine-gun bullet cleave him from head to pelvis.

Less than 20 minutes after hitting the beach, Company 'A' ceased to be an assault company and had become a forlorn little rescue party bent on survival and the saving of the lives of the other men.

The 29th Division was a National Guard Division. The nearest British equivalent would be a Territorial Division. The Americans were pals and many had been since childhood. The leading companies of the 1st Battalion were A, B and D, recruited and based respectively around the Virginian towns of Bedford, Lynchburg and Roanoke.

Veteran John Slaughter told the authors: -

The small town of Bedford lost twenty-three men on D-Day. It's a town of 3,000 people. Twenty-two of those men were from A Company of the 116th Regiment. There were three sets of brothers in A Company. Raymond and Bedford Hoback were killed. Raymond was wounded and lay on the beach. Then when the tide came in he was washed out to sea and drowned. They never found his body. He was carrying a Bible and it washed up upon the sand. The day after D-Day a GI found it. It had Raymond's name and address in Bedford inside and the soldier mailed it to the family. On the Saturday (D-Day was a Tuesday) the family got a telegram that Bedford was killed and then on Sunday they got another one saying that Raymond was too.

This loss of brothers was the inspiration for the Steven Spielberg film. His story was based on an actual family - the Nilands from Buffalo New York, six of whom, four brothers and two cousins, were on active service. Three of the brothers were in Normandy and one of the cousins also jumped at Ste Mère Eglise. When Fritz Niland was asked to identify the body of his brother he was shocked to find it was not the brother he had been told was killed and that he had therefore lost two brothers. They were Sergeant Robert J. Niland of the 505th PIR, 82nd Airborne, killed on 6 June, and 2nd Lieutenant Preston T. Niland of the 22nd Infantry, 4th Division, killed on 7 June. They are buried in the American Cemetery at St Laurent (qv). A third brother was declared missing in the Pacific (but happily was found as a POW after the war).

Further east, at the next draw, designated D3 (there was no D2) and known as *les Moulins* where DOG sector became EASY, the two other battalions of the 116th landed on either side of the exit. There was less opposition on the beach, and smoke from burning grass and buildings produced a screen that saved many lives. On EASY Red though, the 2nd Battalion of the 16th Infantry Regiment of the 1st Division were suffering the same fate as the 1st Battalion of the 116th on DOG Green, having landed opposite the Colleville draw, E3. The Americans, without specialised armoured vehicles for clearing beach obstacles, were confined to single-file movement through the mined areas. This led to slowness in getting off the beaches and to a log-jam of men and material, excellent targets for enemy fire.

Immediately opposite the National Guard Memorial is a small bronze **Plaque** mounted on the wall. It reads (in French) - 'An anti-tank wall blocked this exit from the beach at Vierville. It was destroyed 6.6.44 about 1700 by assault engineers of **29th Div USNG, 121 Battalion**, Company C, 3rd Peloton, 9th Escouade'. They used satchel charges containing 20lbs of plastic explosive.

Perhaps the most telling comment made on D-Day was by Colonel George Taylor of the 'Big Red One' who, on seeing what was happening on the shore, shouted, "Only two kinds of people are staying on this beach - the dead and those who are going to die. Now let's get the blazes out of here." [It is doubtful that he actually said 'blazes'.]

Continue along the beach. To the right is the

• *First American Cemetery in Europe Marker/14.8 miles/5 minutes/Lat & Long: 49.372610 -0.885193*

By house No. 156 the memorial marks the site of the first US burials on Continental Europe. At midnight on 10 June, after 457 bodies had been interred they removed them to St Laurent No 1 (today's US Normandy Cemetery).

Continue to the small plaque in the wall to the left just before the Com Deb Sig.

• *Operation AQUATINT Plaque/15 miles/5 minutes*

The Plaque commemorates an unsuccessful British Commando raid of 1942 by eleven men of the Small Scale Raiding Force commanded by Major Gus March-Phillips. Casualties from the raid are buried in the churchyard of St Laurent-sur-Mer.

Continue to the Comité du Débarquement Monument.

• *Comité du Débarquement Signal Monument/Les Braves Sculpture/15 miles/5 minutes*

On the sides of the Monument are panels to 1st Infantry Division and 116th Infantry Regimental Combat Team of the 29th Infantry Division. The monument marks the junction between DOG and EASY sectors and is at the bottom of Exit D3 les Moulins.

Here the two other battalions of the 116th landed on either side of the exit. An **NTL Totem** also tells the story. On the beach below is a 9m high stainless steel sculpture weighing 15 tons called *Les Braves* by Anilore Ban (website for more details: www.anilorebanon@wanadoo.fr). The central pillar represents The Rise of Freedom and it is flanked by the Wings of Hope and Fraternity. The Euros 600,000 for the statue was donated by M et Mme Jean Paul Delorme. It was inaugurated on 6 June 2004.

Along the beach wall on rue **Bernard Anquetil** (*fusillé*, 1916-1941) are Information Panels describing the symbolism of the sculptures and the Landings here.

'Les Braves' Sculpture,
OMAHA Beach.

Continue along the Beach, signed to le Ruquet, on a road that can be very busy in the season, to the memorials and bunkers on the right.

- ## 2nd Infantry Division/Provisional Engineers Special Brigade Memorials/Bunker, le Ruquet/16.8 miles/10 minutes/Lat & Long: 49.36432 -0.86355

The beach here is EASY Red and the exit which runs uphill past the obvious bunker is E1. The American official history records this as the St Laurent exit and mistakenly calls the river Ruquet, the 'Ruguet'.

OMAHA Memorial
Museum Display.

The bunker was designated WN65 - *Wiederstandsnest 65*. Thanks to the determined efforts of the 37th and 149th Engineer Combat Battalions the 16th Infantry were able to move off the beach here relatively quickly and it became the main exit for OMAHA on D-Day. E Company of the 16th, with the help of the 37th, three of whose men won the DSC that day, took the bunker in a fight that left 40 Germans dead. Serving in the 149th were twin brothers Jay B. Moreland and William W. Moreland, both of whom were killed on D-Day. They are commemorated on the wall in the Garden of the Missing in the American Cemetery. Following its capture, the bunker was used by the **Provisional Engineer Special Brigade Group** as its HQ on D-Day and there is a Plaque on the bunker recording that fact and giving a list of the units in the Brigade.

Over the gun port is another Plaque to the **'467th AAA AW Bn (SP)** [who] landed here am 6 June. Dedicated by the survivors of the Bn June 6 1994.' It was a self-propelled Anti Aircraft Artillery Air Warning Unit.

In front of the bunker is a black monolith Memorial to the **2nd Infantry Division** which was part of the follow-up force on 7 June and on the heights behind and to the left of the bunker can be seen the fir trees that form the boundary to the American National Cemetery.

Below the Memorial is a **NTL Totem** describing how on 7 June the Engineers built an airfield on the flat ground between Le Ruquet and Les Moulins, the first airfield on liberated territory. By 1900 hours that night it was in use to evacuate the wounded.

Return to the Comité Monument and turn left uphill.

To the right is the pleasant **Restaurant l'Omaha** with choice of menus. Tel: +(0)2 31 22 41 46. E-mail: l-omaha@wanadoo.fr.

To the left is the modern, unrated **Hotel-Restaurant D Day House**. Tel: +(0)2 31 92 66 49. E-mail: jj.gaffie@wanadoo.fr Open all year.

Continue to the museum on the right.

• OMAHA MEMORIAL MUSEE, 6 JUIN 1944/17.9 miles/15 minutes/Lat & Long: 49.366995 -0.882003

Now much enlarged, with new dioramas, this private Museum has a chronological presentation of the events from the occupation to the landings, including Operation AQUATINT. There is an impressive display of guns, uniforms and military vehicles from the campaign. Among its well-presented exhibits and documents are many personal items including some moving photos of the 'Bedford Boys' killed on DOG Green Beach and an audio-visual presentation. In the car park is a Sherman Tank, a 155mm 'Long Tom', a landing craft and an **NTL Totem**. There is an attractive boutique.

Open: 15 Feb-15 March 1000-1230 and 1430-1800, 16 March-15 May 0930-1830, 16 May-15 Sept 0930-1900 (July and Aug 0930-1930). 16 Sept-15 Nov 0930-1830. Entrance fee payable. Tel: +(0)2 31 21 97 44. Fax: +(0)2 31 92 72 80. Email: musee-memorial-omaha@wanadoo.fr

Continue to the D514 and turn left. Continue following signs to the American Cemetery. Turn left onto the approach avenue.

Immediately on the left is the charming ***Hotel-Restaurant Domaine de l'Hostréière**, based on an old farmhouse, with 19 well-designed modern bedrooms, heated outdoor pool/sauna, massage, Internet connection. Quick lunches available. Closed 1 Dec-30 April. Tel: +(0)2 31 51 64 64. Fax: +(0)2 31 51 64 65. E-mail: hotelhostreiere@wanadoo.fr

Continue, following signs to the car park and stop at the top as close as possible to the new Visitor/Interpretation Center, a somewhat severe-looking building that belies its contents.

• *The Normandy American Visitor Center, National Cemetery and Memorial, St Laurent/21 miles/1 hour/WC/Lat & Long: 49.357496 - 0.851560*

Open (Visitor Center and Cemetery): 15 April-15 Sept 0900-1800; 16 Sept-14 April 0900-1700. **Closed** Christmas and New Year's Day. Flags are lowered half an hour before closing time when recordings of 'Retreat' and 'To the Color' are played. There is no admission charge. Tel: +(0)2 31 51 62 00. Website: www.abmc.gov

Visitor/Intrepretative Center
This building presents extraordinarily comprehensive audio and visual accounts of the background and realities of the Normandy campaign including such themes as the Deception Plan, Allies, the Airborne, Life Behind the Lines, Resistance, Medical Facilities… There is a deliberate thread throughout to acknowledge the role of the individual whether a Civilian, a Private or a General. There are several films/videos, the principal one being 'Letters', shown on the hour and half hour and lasting 16 minutes in an auditorium that seats 154 and has disabled facilities.

Entry to the Center is via a security check and the exit leads to the cemetery via a serene Hall of Sacrifice. This quite remarkable facility does present a problem to the 'short of time' visitor because it is now a matter of some difficulty to decide whether the Center or the Cemetery should be the main feature. Though not intended as a museum it does act very well in that capacity.

Cemetery Area
The cemetery was built and is maintained by the American Battle Monuments Commission. The ABMC ask that, as this is a place where the dead are honoured, all visitors should show respect during their visit, therefore quiet voices are preferred and appropriate dress (no bare torsos, swimming costumes); no picnics, no dogs outside the car park.

The cemetery, dedicated on 18 July 1956, covers 172.5 acres, all beautifully landscaped and tended, which were donated by the French people 'without charge or taxation'. It contains 9,387 headstones, 307 of whom are unknown and whose white marble crosses or Stars of David (of which there are 149) bear the inscription, 'Here rests in honoured glory a comrade in arms known but to God'. On the known graves is inscribed the rank, unit, name, date of death and home state of the serviceman or woman commemorated.

Medal of Honor recipients' headstones are lettered in gold. This is America's highest award for gallantry, the equivalent of the British Victoria Cross. The most famous is that of **Brigadier General Theodore Roosevelt** (Plot D, Row 28, Grave 45), who died of a heart

The Reflective Pool, Normandy American Cemetery, St Laurent.

attack on 12 July 1944. Beside him lies his youngest brother, Lieutenant Quentin Roosevelt, a World War I aviator who died in France on 14 July 1918, and who was re-interred here when the cemetery was made.

There are forty other pairs of brothers, 33 of whom lie side by side, including the **Nilands** (qv) in Plot F, Row 15, graves 11 and 12. Eight other pairs of brothers are buried here, but in different rows, and a father and son, **Colonel Ollie Reed** (Plot E, Row 20, Grave 19) and **Ollie Reed Junior** (Grave 20). Cousins **Paul A. Lepisto and Tauno J. Lepisto** lie together (Plot E, Row 18, Graves 8 and 9).

Two other **Medals of Honor** recipients of the Normandy campaign buried in the cemetery are: **Tech Sergeant Frank Peregory** (qv) of the 116th Infantry Regiment, 29th Division and **1st Lieutenant Jimmie W. Monteith**, Jr. of the 16th Infantry, 1st Division whose act of conspicuous gallantry took place on 6 June on OMAHA.

There are also some women Red Cross personnel and WACs (**Mary Bankston Pfc**, D-20-46; **Mary Barlow Pfc**, A-19-30; **Dolores Brown**, Sgt, F-13-19; **Elizabeth Richardson**, Red Cross, A-21-5. Elizabeth was a 'Doughnut Dolly', giving out coffee, doughnuts, chewing gum, newspapers from a bus that drove among military units. She died in a

plane crash on the way to a Red Cross meeting on 25 July 1945.) Also buried here (Plot G, Row 14, Grave 12) is **Major Thomas Howie**, 29th Div, who motivated his troops with the cry, 'I'll see you in St Lô' as they battled to liberate the town. The servicemen and women resting here were re-interred from temporary cemeteries (e.g. at Ste Mère Eglise, la Cambe and OMAHA Beach - now marked by memorials). 14,000 others of their comrades were repatriated at government expense. This impressive cemetery receives more than 1 million visitors each year - not only veterans or their families, but local French people. It was the setting for the beginning and end of the film *Saving Private Ryan*.

Other features are:

Time Capsule. Embedded in the ground on the right-hand side just inside the old entrance, the time capsule, dedicated to General Eisenhower, contains sealed reports of the 6 June 1944 landings. It is to be opened 6 June 2044.

Memorial. This area consists of a semi-circular colonnade, with stone loggias at each side which are engraved with vivid battle maps, picked out in coloured enamel and designed by Robert Foster of New York. Ornamental urns at each side flank a 22ft-high bronze statue of *The Spirit of American Youth Rising from the Waves*, sculpted by Donald de Lue of New York.

In 1987 the American Veterans' Association donated a memorial bell which tolls every hour and at noon. Every hour the carillon tolls the time and plays two US patriotic songs at random.

Garden of the Missing. Behind the memorial, the garden's semi-circular wall bears the names of 1,557 missing with no known graves, who came from 49 of the 50 States that make up the Union. An asterisk against a name means that the person has since been identified, two of the eleven, **Jay and William Moreland** (qv), were twin brothers

Reflective Pool/Stars and Stripes. In front of the memorial is the rectangular reflective pool with water lilies and, beyond it, two enormous flagstaffs. The American flag flies proudly from each of them, raised each morning, lowered each evening.

Orientation Tables. Overlooking the beach (OMAHA) beyond the memorial is an orientation table with a map pointing to features nearby. From here one can descend a deceptively gentle-looking path down to the beach itself. (It seems very long and steep on the way up).

On the way down, a second orientation table shows the Mulberry Harbour designed for OMAHA, washed away in the storm of 19 June.

Chapel. Along the central pathway is the non-denominational chapel with a fine ceiling mosaic designed by Leon Kroll of New York

Statues of United States and France. At the end of the main axis beyond the chapel are two granite figures sculpted by Donald de Lue representing the two countries.

End of Itinerary Two

[OR you may wish to visit the Big Red One Assault Museum at Colleville-sur-Mer. Lat & Long: 49.347390 -0.850203

This may be reached by returning to the D514 and continuing east some half a mile.
This small privately owned (by knowledgeable enthusiast Pierre-Louis Gosselin) museum concentrates on the US 1st Inf Div with many rare artefacts, debris, ephemera, mostly donated by the men or their families. The personal theme makes it extremely moving. Open: every day except Tues June-Aug 1000-19000, Sept, Oct, Nov, March 1000-1200 and 1400-1800. It's wise to phone first. Tel: +(0)2 31 21 53 81, E-mail: bigredoneassaultmuseum@gmail/.com Entrance fee payable.]

ITINERARY THREE

BAYEUX, ARROMANCHES & GOLD BEACH

The background information given here covers the whole 2nd (British) Army plan. The actions on GOLD, the beach adjacent to Arromanches, are then described, in conjunction with a battlefield tour.

The 2nd Army

The Supreme Commander had three subordinate Commanders in Chief - for the sea, the air and the land. Although General Montgomery was never formally appointed C-in-C Land Forces, that was in effect his position. Under his command were four armies, known collectively as 21st Army Group. They were divided as follows:

Assault armies	First (US) Army	General Bradley
	Second (British) Army	General Dempsey
Follow-up armies	Third (US) Army	General Patton
	First (Canadian) Army	General Crerar

The British Second Army's part in the plan was 'to make straight for Caen to establish the pivot while 6th Airborne Division was given the task of seizing the crossings over the Caen canal and of operating on our extreme left.'

The Second Army's seaborne element was made up from two Corps: XXX Corps under General G.C. Bucknall, landing on GOLD Beach, and 1st Corps under General Dempsey landing on JUNO and SWORD Beaches.

The preparatory fire-plan of bomber strikes, naval bombardment and tactical fighter support was common along all beaches, though timings varied slightly to allow for the different H-Hours occasioned by the variation in tide from west to east. However, there was one major difference in assault tactics between the American and British beaches, and that was in the use of the specialised armour of the 79th Armoured Division to provide close support to the assaulting infantry. The British had it, and generally the Americans did not.

The range of equipment (known generally as 'Hobart's Funnies' after General Hobart who promoted the idea) produced was extraordinary and with a colourful vocabulary to match:

DD Tanks: floating ('Donald Duck') Duplex Drive M4 Sherman tanks. Engine power could be transferred from the tracks to twin propellers and, by erecting high canvas screens all around, it could float. Once on shore, power was returned to the tracks and the screen jettisoned.

Crocodiles: mainly Churchill tanks modified to be flamethrowers.

Crabs: generally a standard M4 Sherman tank fitted with an extended pair of arms carrying a flail. Its purpose was to clear minefields by beating the mines into explosion - a sort of military Hoover, beating, sweeping and cleaning at 1 1/2 mph.

BARV: Beach Armoured Recovery Vehicle, usually, but not invariably, a Sherman. The gun turret was replaced by a superstructure allowing the tank to drive into deep water and through fitted winches or small dozer blades it was able to clear beaches of stranded vehicles.

Petard: an AVRE (Armoured Vehicle Royal Engineers) based on a Churchill chassis with its normal main armament replaced by a 290mm short-barrelled mortar which fired a 40lb 'flying dustbin' explosive charge to destroy enemy pillboxes and fixed obstructions.

Bobbin: a normal Churchill tank adapted to carry a 110-yard long spool of flexible coir coconut matting that could be laid in front of the vehicle to form a road over soft or slippery ground for itself and following vehicles.

ARK: 'Armoured Ramp Carrier', a turretless Churchill tank carrying two runways across its flat top. It could be used to provide a ramped road up and over a beach wall or could be dropped into ditches or streams to form a bridge.

AVRE: 'Armoured Vehicle Royal Engineers'. This is a generic title for a whole range of specialised armoured vehicles. They include those above, plus others carrying huge 2-ton bundles of wood called fascines used to fill holes in roadways, bridge-layers, craned recovery vehicles, etc.

GOLD BEACH LANDINGS - 50th NORTHUMBRIAN DIVISION

Assault Time:	0725 hours
Leading Formations:	8th Armoured Brigade DD tanks
	6th Battalion, The Green Howards.
	5th Battalion, East Yorkshire Regiment
	1st Battalion, Dorset Regiment
	1st Battalion, Royal Hampshire Regiment
50th Division Commander:	Major General D.A.H. Graham
Bombarding Force K:	Cruisers: HMS *Orion*
	HMS *Ajax*
	HMS *Argonaut*
	HMS *Emerald*
	Gunboat: HNMS *Flores* (Dutch)
	13 destroyers including ORP *Krakowiak* (Polish)
German Defenders:	716th Division
	352nd Division
352nd Div Commander:	Lieutenant General Dietrich Kraiss
716th Div Commander:	Lieutenant General Wilhelm Richter

The Plan - GOLD Beach Landings

The D-Day mission of the 50th Northumbrian Division was complicated. It was to capture Bayeux, to establish a bridgehead across the N13 Bayeux to Caen road, to take the German gun battery at Longues and to establish contact with flanking formations. This latter involved the capture of Port-en-Bessin to link up with Americans from OMAHA Beach.

GOLD beach was subdivided into JIG and KING sectors. The divisional plan was that the 231st Brigade would land on JIG east of le Hamel (Asnelles), clear the village and then drive along the coast towards the Americans at Port-en-Bessin, the latter having been taken by commandos from the rear. The 69th Brigade was to land on KING west of la Rivière (Ver-sur-Mer) and to head inland towards the N13 Bayeux to Caen road. The leading brigades were thus moving apart. Into the gap between them at 1000 hours were to come two follow-up brigades, the 56th and the 151st. Their task was to take Bayeux.

What Happened on D-Day

The weather was bad, probably at its worst, opposite GOLD Beach. So rough was the sea that it was decided that the DD tanks, scheduled to land ahead of the infantry and to be launched some 7,000 yards out, would not be launched until within 700 yards of the beach.

The leading formations touched down within a minute or two of their allotted time and at the right place. At le Hamel a German strongpoint held out until noon, causing considerable casualties by raking the beach with machine-gun fire. At la Rivière the preliminary bombardment had been very effective and there was relatively little opposition The reserve and follow-up formations were landed successfully and, while not

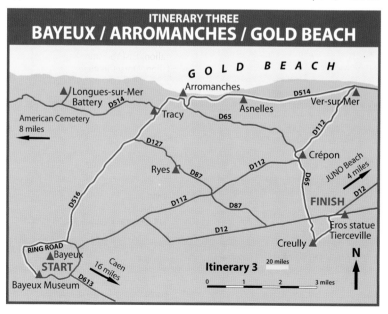

ITINERARY THREE
BAYEUX / ARROMANCHES / GOLD BEACH

all of the D-Day objectives had been achieved, by the end of the day the 50th Division beachhead measured six miles by six, the N13 was in sight, reconnaissance patrols had entered the outskirts of Bayeux and No 47 Royal Marine Commando were on the heights above Port-en-Bessin. Although there had not been any contact with the Americans from OMAHA Beach in the west, contact had been established with the Canadians from JUNO Beach in the east.

THE BATTLEFIELD TOUR

THE TOUR STARTS AT THE BAYEUX MUSEE MEMORAL DE LA BATAILLE DE NORMANDIE

* Planned duration without stops or extra visits: 5 hours
* Total distance: 19.8 miles

Follow signs to Bayeux from the Autoroute A13 – (Exit 36 from the Caen direction or Exit 37 from Cherbourg) and take the inner ring road south to the Museum. **Set your mileometer to zero.** *The free car park is useful for the next visit to the British cemetery.*

Bayeux

This historical city was one of the D-Day objectives of 50th Northumbrian Division landing on GOLD Beach, and reconnaissance patrols of the 151st Brigade entered its outskirts at about 2030 hours on the evening of 6 June.

There is no disputing Bayeux's claim to be the first major town to be liberated. By midday on 7 June members of 56th Brigade and tanks were entering the city. Miraculously its historic treasures - the cathedral, the ancient and picturesque buildings - were all spared the fearful damage that many Norman towns endured. The precious Bayeux Tapestry had long since been removed and was hidden in the Château de Sourches near Le Mans.

At 1530 hours on 14 June a car with a loudspeaker raced through the narrow streets blazoning the marvellous news that Général de Gaulle was in France and would address the citizens at the Place du Château (now renamed Place Gén de Gaulle) in half an hour. The moment is crystallised for posterity as a striking *bas relief* on the Liberation Memorial, Rond Point de Vaucelles - see below.

• *Musée Mémorial de la Bataille de Normandie/MPs, Notts Yeomanry & 2nd Bn Essex Regt Memorials/0 miles/45 minutes (add 25 minutes for the film)/RWC/Lat & Long: 49.272800 -0.711129*

In the parking area is a blue **NTL Totem**. The Museum, owned and administered by the *Mairie* of Bayeux is more '*pédagogique*' (educational) in presentation than most and exhibits are chosen so as not to cause offence. It covers the period from D-Day to the end of August 1944 in a series of thematic presentations including a 25 minute film e.g. Resistance, Airstrips, Medical Services etc with the minimum use of archival equipment or material. There is also a documentation section and a boutique selling books and souvenirs.

Open: 1 May-30 Sept 0930-1830. 1 Oct-30 April 1000-1230 and 1400-1800. Entrance fee payable (except for Veterans, Service personnel in uniform and local schoolchildren). Tel: +(0)2 31 51 46 90.   Fax: +(0)2 31 51 46 91   E-mail: bataillenormandie@mairie-bayeux.fr Website: www.mairie-bayeux.fr WCs and snack-dispensing machines and ample free parking, which should also be used for the Cemetery and Memorial.

Outside are a number of vehicles, guns and some sadly deteriorating tanks (including a Hetzer SP anti-tank gun, a Sherman tank, a Churchill AVRE, and a 40mm Bofors gun).

In September 1993 a **Memorial** was unveiled in the grounds to the **Notts (Sherwood Rangers) Yeomanry**, one of whose A Squadron tank troops commanded by Lt Mike Howden was the first to enter the city on the evening of 6 June. On 7 June 2002, in a project costing some £35,000, a **Memorial** was unveiled to the 2nd Bn, the Essex Regiment ('The Pompadours'). In the line of memorials is also one to the **Corps of Military Police** and a **MLC Marker** erected in 2004.

Leave your car in the museum car park and walk up the road towards the CWGC Cemetery or follow signs to the **Memorial Garden to War Reporters**. *By the entrance is a stone memorial to the famous war photographer,* **Frank Capa**. *There is no parking at the Cemetery/Memorial and the area between them is now paved.*

• Bayeux Commonwealth War Graves Commission Memorial and Cemetery/30 minutes

On the same side of the road as the Museum is the Bayeux Memorial to the Missing with No Known Graves, designed by Philip Hepworth. It bears the names of 1,805 Commonwealth service men and women (1,534 from Britain, 270 from Canada and 1 from South Africa) who fell in the Battle of Normandy.

The Latin inscription above reads *'NOS A GULIELMO VICTI VICTORIS PATRIAM LIBERAVIMUS' (WE WHO WERE CONQUERED BY WILLIAM LIBERATE HIS FATHERLAND).*

Over the road is the beautifully maintained cemetery - the largest British World War II cemetery in France. It contains 4,648 graves - 3,935 from the United Kingdom, 181 from Canada, 17 from Australia, 8 from New Zealand, 1 from South Africa, 25 from Poland, 3 from France, 2 from Czechoslovakia, 2 from Italy, 7 from Russia, 466 from Germany and 1 unidentified. Each non-Commonwealth nationality has a differently shaped top to its stones. In the shelter to the left of the stone of remembrance the cemetery register and the visitors' book are housed in a bronze box. Please sign.

One of the burials of note is that of **Cpl Sidney Bates**, 1st Battalion the Norfolk Regiment, who won the **VC** for an action on 6 August involving 10th SS Panzer Division on the Periers Ridge (qv).

Return to your car and take the D5 inner ring road, direction Cherbourg to the roundabout by the Novotel Hotel. ***Hotel Novotel**, Rond Point de Vaucelles. 77 rooms. Heated outdoor pool. Highly recommended. Tel: +(0)2 31 92 16 11. E-mail: ho964@accor.com.

In the middle of the roundabout is the **Bayeux Liberation Memorial** depicting General de Gaulle's visit of 14 June 1944 and in the grassed centre is the holder for the Flame of Liberty. Here each 16th September since 1945 young people come from Eindhoven in Holland, the first major Dutch city liberated, to rekindle the Flame of Liberty and Friendship.

Musée Mémorial de la Bataille de Normandie.

Continue around the roundabout following the D613 inner ring road and signs to Arromanches. Turn left on the D516 and continue to the parking area beside the D Day Landings Museum (Musée du Débarquement). There is a 'buy your own ticket' parking meter and a uniformed attendant to make sure that you use it.

On entering Arromanches, pass on the left the ****Hotel Chanteclair**. 22 rooms. Tel: +(0)2 31 21 38 97. E-mail: hotelchanteclair@aol.com

CWGC Cemetery, Bayeux.

BAYEUX WAR CEMETERY

Arromanches

The town was liberated on the afternoon of D-Day by the 1st Battalion Royal Hampshire Regiment who had landed on GOLD Beach and descended upon the German defenders from the heights of St Côme to the east.

Arromanches is remembered for the harbour that was towed across the English Channel - the **Mulberry**. The idea is said to have originated in a memo from Sir Winston Churchill to Vice-Admiral Mountbatten Chief of Combined Operations on 30 May 1942. It ran:

> **'PIERS FOR USE ON BEACHES**
> They must float up and down with the tide. The anchor problem must be mastered. Let me have the best solution worked out. Don't argue the matter. The difficulties will argue for themselves.'

Two transportable harbours each roughly the size of that at Dover were designed. One was to be for the Americans at OMAHA Beach, the other for the British at Arromanches. The basic concept was simple. First a line of sixty old ships would be sunk off all five beaches to provide an elemental breakwater. These ships were called 'Gooseberries'. Inside the **Gooseberries**, off OMAHA Beach and Arromanches, a huge semi-circle of hollow concrete boxes, called caissons and codenamed **Phoenixes**, would be towed across the Channel and sunk to form a harbour wall.

The first Phoenix arrived at Arromanches at dawn on 9 June and by 18 June 115 had been sunk in a huge 5-mile-long arc around the town, but thirteen days after D-Day a storm destroyed the OMAHA harbour. The Arromanches harbour survived, battered but serviceable. The gale caused more damage in three days than the Germans did in two weeks. The town calls itself 'Arromanches Port Winston' and has adopted a coat of arms showing the British Lion and the American Eagle breaking the chains of occupation.

Musée du Débarquement, Arromanches.

• D-Day Landings Museum/RE (Transportation) Memorial/Supporting Services, LST & Landing Craft, 2nd Cheshires Plaques/Brig Gen Stanier Memorial, Arromanches/7.3 miles/60 minutes/RWC/Lat & Long: 49.3402 -0.620928

The Museum, the *Exposition Permanente du Débarquement*, was opened by Président René Coty in 1954. It has a working model of the Landing Beaches, a model of the Mulberry Harbour, a diorama of the landings, a variety of documentary exhibits and a film of the construction of Port Winston. Commentaries are given in French, English, Spanish, Italian, Dutch and German. This important Museum is the focal point of the British Landing Beaches where it is possible to overlook the remains of Mulberry Phoenixes while listening to their story. There is a good book/souvenir shop in the Museum.

Outside are a number of artillery pieces and a Sherman tank on the hill behind.

Open: Feb, Nov, Dec 1000-1230 and 1330-1700. March and Oct 0930-1230 and 1330-1730. April: 0900-1230 and 1330-1800. May - Aug 0900-1900. Sept 0900-1800. Closed Jan and 24, 25, 26 and 31 Dec. Tel: +(0)2 31 22 34 31. Fax: +(0)2 31 92 68 83. E-mail: info.arromanches@normandy1944.com

Inside the entrance is a **Plaque to the 2nd Cheshires**. Outside to the left of the museum entrance is a bronze and granite **Memorial to the Transportation Branch of the Royal Engineers**. On the wall below the Memorial are **Plaques** to the **Supporting Services, LST and Landing Craft** and to the **Merchant Navy**.

On the sea wall is a **Memorial to General Sir Alexander Stanier Bt**. [sic] 231st Brigade, 50th Division, 1899-1995. *'Libérateur d'Arromanches le 6 juin 1944.'*

Around the museum parking area is a variety of hotels (e.g. ****Hotel de la Marine**, 2 Quai de Canada. 28 rooms. Open 11 Feb-11 Nov. Tel: +(0)2 31 22 34 19. E-mail: hotel.de.la.marine@wanadoo.fr Excellent restaurant and sea view. ***Hotel de Normandie**, 5 Place 6 Juin in the main square. 21 rooms. Tel: +(0)2 31 22 34 32, E-mail: contact@hotel-de-normandie.fr ****Le Mountbatten**, 20 Bvd Gilbert Longuet. 9 rooms. Tel: +(0)2 31 22 50 30. E-mail: mountbattenhotel@wanadoo.fr) restaurants/souvenir shops, and just along the road running beyond it is the **TOURIST OFFICE**, 4 rue du Mal Joffre,Tel: +(0)2 31 22 36 45. Fax: +(0)2 31 22 92 06. E-mail off-tour@mail.cpod.fr

> Leave Arromanches eastward on the D514 coast road, following signs to Courseulles/Cinéma Circulaire and stop in the parking area (for which there is a fee in the season) on the left just past the Statue of the Virgin Mary on the cliffs above the town.

• St Côme de Fresne Table d'Orientation/Bunker/RE Memorial/ Free French Airforce Memorial/360o Film/8.1 miles/30 minutes

By the cliff edge are the remains of German bunkers which contained field guns which menaced GOLD Beach (to the right) and were silenced by HMS *Belfast*. In the sea, the remains of the Arromanches Mulberry Harbour can be seen, and to the left below is Arromanches itself. This position, and Arromanches, were taken by the Hampshires before 2100 hours on D-Day.

No 47 RM Commando landed to your right on GOLD Beach, just below these heights, and swung around behind you going to your left, heading for Port-en-Bessin, a 10-mile march away, due west.

The ***table d'orientation*** by the parking area gives excellent views over the remains of the Mulberry Harbour. Near it are traces of the radar station destroyed by allied airforce raids a few weeks before OVERLORD. There is a **NTL Totem** beside it.

*Walk towards the 360° Cinema to the memorial with the badge of the **Free French Airforce**. Continue to*

The **RE Memorial** on the left with a fine display of unit badges. Well forward in the beach assault forces had to be engineer units equipped to clear whatever devices the Germans had put up. The Corps Royal Engineers plan identified its tasks as follows: -

On the beaches - obstacle clearance, construction of exits and subsequent beach organisation

Operations inland - bridging, airfields and routes. The importance that the British attached to the engineers and to Hobart's Funnies, which were operated by them, is well illustrated by the planned landing sequence given in the orders for the landing of 8th Infantry Brigade Group at la Brêche (visited later). It was: -

A and B Squadrons 13/18 Hussars (DD tanks)

Eight gapping teams, each of two flail tanks, three AVREs, one bulldozer and two obstacle clearing teams

The assaulting infantry.

The **360° Cinema** presentation uses an original 'Circorama' process employing 9 synchronised cameras to give a unique and moving account of the events of 6 June 1944. It has a good book and souvenir shop. **Open:** every day June, July, August 0940-1840. May, September 1010-1740. Feb, March, April, Oct, Nov, Dec 1010-1640. Shows at 10 and 40 minutes past each hour. Entrance fee payable. Tel: +(0)2 31 22 30 30. Email: contact@arromanches360.com

Continue on the D514 downhill.

On the wall of the Church of St Côme that is passed on the right is a **Plaque** commemorating the ringing of the bells as soon as the Allies landed.

Continue to the crossroads with the D205 just east of le Hamel (Asnelles). Stop and walk 100 yards down the small road to the sea.

• D514/D205 La Guerre Crossroads/9.1 miles/10 minutes/OP

At low tide there is a good view of the remaining Phoenixes of the Arromanches Mulberry, built to last a hundred days and still around after the Millenium. This was the eastern end of the Mulberry, the western was at Tracy. There is a typical German shore bunker with deadly fields of fire across the open beaches.

The 1st Battalion Royal Hampshires landed on the beach here and to the east (right), accompanied by DD tanks and Hobart's Funnies. With the armour ahead of them as they jumped from their landing craft, the soldiers of the Hampshires had the firepower to cover their movement across the sands. But the German fire was heavy and the first three CRABS which flailed their way up the beach were bogged down or stopped by an anti-tank gun and both the CO and the 2nd in Command of the Hampshires became casualties early on. It was not until after midday that the area was cleared.

Continue on the D514 to the crossroads in the centre of Asnelles where the D514 meets the Rue de Southampton. Stop by the memorials on the left.

• Asnelles/Place Alexander Stanier/50th Division, SW Borderers Memorials/Gen de Gaulle Message/9.5 miles/10 minutes

The crossroads area is known as 'Place Alexander Stanier', in honour of the commander of the 231st Infantry Brigade of the **50th Northumbrian Division**, Sir Alexander Stanier Bart (sic), DSO MC. At the small road 'Rue The Devonshire Regiment', there is a **Memorial** to the division, the leading brigade of the 231st, and three battalions - the 2nd Battalion **Devonshire Regiment**, the 1st Battalion **Hampshire Regiment** and the 1st Battalion the **Dorset Regiment**. The Dorsets, working in conjunction with a variety of AVREs, were off the beach here within the hour and met members of No 47 RM Commando. By nightfall they had reached Ryes, three miles inland. A Memorial surmounted by a metal Cross of Lorraine reproduces **Général de Gaulle's message** of June 1940 and a black marble Memorial with inscriptions in English, French and Welsh commemorates the 2nd Battalion the **South Wales Borderers** who landed at Asnelles on 6 June 1944.

From Place Alexander Stanier turn left in front of the Memorial to Nos Glorieux Libérateurs and at the first crossroads turn left down the small road to the sea. Stop in the car park.

Ahead is a significant **Bunker** on which are **Memorial Plaques to the Essex Yeomanry and the 147th (Essex Yeomanry) Field Regiment, RA**. The Essex and the Sherwoods came ashore at 0730 with Sherman DD tanks and Sextons, supporting the Hampshires and the Dorsets and were given much trouble by this blockhouse which was eventually knocked out by Sergeant R. E. Palmer, using a 25-pounder self-propelled gun at 300 yards, in an action that won him the Military Medal. There is a **NTL Totem** beside the Bunker.

Return to the D514 and continue. At the small crossroads just after the sign indicating that you are entering Ver-sur-Mer, stop.

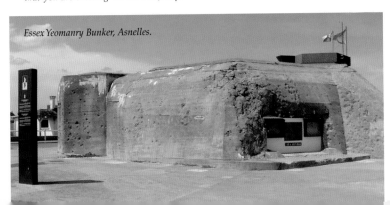

Essex Yeomanry Bunker, Asnelles.

King Sector GOLD Beach exit road on D+1

King Sector GOLD Beach exit road today.

• KING Sector, GOLD Beach and Stan Hollis VC Memorial/12.5 miles/5 minutes/OP

Stand at the crossroads.

The road to your left leading towards you from the sea was the exit road from King Sector of GOLD Beach (see contemporary and modern photos above). It was up this road that CSM Hollis with D Coy of the 6th Bn the Green Howards advanced on D-Day. The leading vehicle in the contemporary photo is a Cromwell tank, the second vehicle, a Sherman, is exactly at the crossroads where you are now.

At the beach end of this road is a **Memorial** on an old tram hut to **CSM Stan Hollis** of the Green Howards which was unveiled by his son on 8 June 2006. CSM Hollis, with whom one of the authors was privileged to tour the area, was the only man to win a **VC** on D Day.

The main enemy position here was known as the Fleury battery and consisted of four 150mm guns in concrete casemates on Mont Fleury. It was situated in what is now a new housing estate half a mile to the right uphill from where you are. The casemates are still there today, though steadily being masked by new houses.

Sexton SP, Ver-sur-Mer.

The assault of the 69th Brigade was led by the 6th Battalion Green Howards under Lieutenant-Colonel Robin Hastings accompanied by a squadron of the 4th/7th Royal Dragoon Guards with DD tanks, two teams of AVRE and flail tanks (CRABS), one platoon of medium machine-guns of the 2nd Cheshire Regiment and a detachment of Royal Engineers. At 0730 hours the leading companies began their final approach to the beach. Overhead thundered the express train shells from HMS *Warspite*, accompanied by the smaller calibre fire of cruisers and destroyers. 25-pounders of the Royal Artillery, firing from landing craft, added their enthusiasm to the affair and in the last few yards came the dragon's roar of the rocket ships, 100 yards out, firing four salvos a minute of ninety rockets each.

'D' Company, who had been given the task of taking the Fleury battery, suffered a number of casualties on landing. The company commander, Major R. Lofthouse, rallied his men in conjunction with his CSM, Stan Hollis, and personally led them off the beach and up the road you can see. For that and the actions that followed he was awarded the Military Cross and **CSM Hollis** the **VC**. His citation reads:

In Normandy, on June 6th, 1944, during the assault on the beaches and the Mont Fleury battery, CSM Hollis's Company Commander noticed that two of the pill-boxes had been by-passed, and went with CSM Hollis to see that they were clear. When they were twenty yards from the pill-box a machine-gun opened fire from the slit, and CSM Hollis instantly rushed straight at the pill-box, recharged his magazine, threw a grenade in through the door, and fired his Sten gun into it, killing two Germans and making the remainder prisoner. He then cleared several Germans from a neighbouring trench. By his action he undoubtedly saved his Company from being fired on heavily from the rear, and enabled them to open the main beach exit. Later the same day, in the village of Crépon, the Company encountered a field gun and crew, armed with Spandaus, at a hundred yards' range. CSM Hollis was put in command of a party to cover an attack on the gun, but the movement was held up. Seeing this, CSM Hollis pushed right forward to engage the gun with a PIAT [Projector Infantry Anti-tank] from a house at fifty yards' range. He was observed by a sniper who fired and grazed his right cheek, and at the same moment the gun swung round and fired at point blank range into the house. To avoid the falling masonry CSM Hollis moved his party to an alternative position. Two of the enemy gun crew had by this time been killed, and the gun was destroyed shortly afterwards. He later found that two of his men had stayed behind in the house, and immediately volunteered to get them out. In full view of the enemy, who were continually firing at him, he went forward alone using a Bren gun to distract their attention from the other men. Under cover of his diversion the two men were able to get back. Wherever fighting was heaviest CSM Hollis appeared, and in the course of a magnificent day's work he displayed the utmost gallantry, and on two separate occasions his courage and initiative prevented the enemy from holding up the advance at critical stages. It was largely through his heroism and resource that the Company's objectives were gained and casualties were not heavier, and by his own bravery he saved the lives of many of his men.

Continue, ignoring signs to the Green Howard's Memorial which will be visited later, to the cross-roads in Ver-sur-Mer.

• Memorials to 2nd Herts and RA, Admiral Ramsay House, Sexton SP, Ver-sur-Mer/13.0 miles/10 minutes

This is KING sector, the extreme eastern end of GOLD beach. Here the East Yorkshire Regiment landed alongside the Green Howards, followed by the Hertfordshires. (The D514 continues into JUNO, Love sector.)

The road leading to the beach is Avénue Colonel J.R. Harper and on the corner is a **Memorial** to the battalion he commanded, the **2nd Battalion Hertfordshire Regiment**. Almost opposite, a few yards along the D514 towards JUNO, is a substantial **house used by Admiral Sir Bertram Ramsay**, Allied Naval Commander in Chief, as a headquarters and there is a memorial **Plaque** on the gate post. An impressive **Memorial** on the opposite corner commemorating the **Royal Artillery** of the 50th Northumbrian Division was dedicated in September 1993.

On the right in Espace Robert Kiln is a **Sexton SP 25-pounder gun**, of the type used in the landings at Ver. It was presented by Dr Kiln the son of Ver veteran Maj Robert Kiln who died in 1997.

Turn right on the Avénue du 6 juin, the D112, direction Crépon and continue to Ver.
Turn right following Centre Ville/Musée signs to the T junction.

100 yards to the right at this junction can be seen a sign pointing to the left to Résidence Les Loges. 100 yards along that road is a blockhouse of the Fleury Battery.

Turn left (this is the D112) and next left to the America Museum on Rue America and stop in the Museum car park in Place Amiral Byrd.

• America-GOLD Beach Museum, Ver-sur-Mer/13.9 miles/15 minutes/Lat & Long: 49.33658 -0.52519

The name 'America' refers to the first airmail from New York to France in June 1927 forced down here because of thick fog over Paris. It is ironic that the only museum behind this British beach is called 'America'. The museum commemorates the assaults by the 69th Brigade and the 50th Northumbrian Division at Ver-sur-Mer. There is a video theatre in the basement. **Open:** 1030-1330 and 1430-1730 every day July-August. May, June, September and October closed on Tuesday. Entrance fee payable. Tel: +(0)2 31 22 58 58. E-mail: jean-pierre122@wanadoo.fr

In the square is a **NTL Totem** and in the garden in the centre is an anchor from a 1944 battleship, recovered in 1985. To the left on House No 22 is a **Plaque** to the old Hotel America, residence of officers of the **Staff of 9th Beach Gp RM** from 6 June-30 July 1944. These officers under Col J.R. Harper called it 'The Gold Inn'.

Return to the D112, wiggling out of Ver and turn left following signs to Crépon.

(Above) *America-GOLD Museum, Ver-sur-Mer.*

Green Howards Memorial, Crépon.

Detail, 4th/7th RDG Memorial, Cruelly.

On entering Crépon follow Autres Directions to the roundabout and turn left on the D65 to the figure of a seated soldier, some 400m further on the left.

• Green Howards Memorial/16.3 miles/10 minutes/Lat & Long: 49.31574 -0.55000

The figure on this magnificent Memorial is popularly supposed to be that of CSM Stanley Hollis VC but the figure (sculpted by James Butler) represents a soldier of the Green Howards reflecting upon the events of the 6th June 1944. The Memorial, which cost around £100,000 bears the legend, 'Remember the 6th June 1944', and is dedicated 'To the memory of all the Green Howards who fought and died in the Second World War'. The memorial was unveiled on 26 October 1996 by HM Harald V, King of Norway, Colonel-in-Chief of the Green Howards. Built on a site provided by the people of Crépon, the Memorial is one of the most beautiful in the whole Normandy area.

Beside the Memorial are Information Panels and in the churchyard here are two RAF graves from 10 June 1944: **Aircraftsman 1st Class David D. Harris and Cpl Frank Olney**. They were both 23.

Continue on the D65. In one-third of a mile on the right is
*** Chateaux & Hotels de France/Logis de France **Hotel-Restaurant Ferme de la**

Rançonnière. Lat & Long: 49.31144 - 0.54719 Tel: +(0)2 31 22 21 73. E-mail: _hotel@ranconniere.com_ Website: _www.ranconniere.com_ . Hotel open all year. 35 rooms. Restaurant closed January. Picturesque traditional 13th Century Normandy manor house.

Opposite is an **Information Panel** describing nearby **Airstrip B2** with many contemporary photos and the Depot set up in the Farm by 9th Beach No 2 Detail, RASC. In the large concrete hangar adjacent to the hotel a Base Post Office was set up.

Continue to the crossroads with the D12, go straight over, down the narrow road, and stop just before the bridge over the River Seulles. Look back to your right.

Eros, RE Memorial, Tierceville.

• The Château at Creullet/18.3 miles/5 minutes

It was here on 9 June that **General Montgomery** parked his caravan and set up his Tactical HQ. He met **Winston Churchill** and **Field Marshal Smuts** in the grand salon of the château on 12 June, **de Gaulle** on 14 June and **King George VI** on 16 June. There is a **Memorial Plaque** on the gateway pillar.

The road that you have followed from Crépon, the D65, is the one taken by the 4th/7th Royal Dragoon Guards on D-Day after landing on GOLD Beach KING sector with the Green Howards. In the early evening the 4th/7th lost four tanks on approaching the river Seulles.

Continue over the river. Stop at the memorial on the left.

• 4th/7th Royal Dragoon Guards Memorial/18.6 miles/5 minutes

Creully was on the regimental centre line and was liberated by 'A' Squadron on 6 June after fierce fighting, although there was no fighting in the town itself. The Memorial, designed by Sir Peter Shepheard, was unveiled on 6 June 1992 by HRH the Duke of Kent, Colonel-in-Chief of the Regiment.

Continue uphill (past the Old Mill on the River Seulles) and turn left by the French 'Poilu' World War One Memorial into the square in Creully.

• Creully Château BBC Studio and Plaque/18.7 miles/15 minutes/ RWC

The BBC set up a studio here on 19 June and it was used by American, Canadian and French broadcasters. The tower may be climbed and it contains a small museum.

Open: 1 July-15 September only 1030-1230 and 1430-1730 Tues-Fri. Tel: +(0)2 31 80 67 08. Fax: +(0)2 31 80 66 98. Entrance fee payable. Guided tours in English and French. If closed ask at the **TOURIST OFFICE**, 12 Place Edmond Paillaud. Tel: + (0)2 31 80 67 08. E-mail: tourisme.creully@wanadoo.fr

There are a couple of restaurants in this attractive little town, (including the Logis de France ** **Hostellerie St-Martin**, 6 Place Edmond Paillaud with its restaurant in an old 16th Century vaulted hall. 12 rooms. Tel: +(0)2 31 80 10 11. E-mail: hostellerie.st.martin@wanadoo.fr) and a useful supermarket. The church is historic and interesting.

Continue straight through Creully on the D93 towards Tierceville. On meeting the D12 turn right and drive about one hundred yards to the roundabout where there is a memorial.

• Tierceville Eros/19.8 miles/5 minutes/LAT 7 Long: 49.29496 -0.52735

This copy of Eros, made in cement, was constructed by **179 Special Field Company RE**, on 23 August 1944. As this area became an RE enclave the statue probably commemorates the Royal Engineers in general.

• End of Itinerary Three

ITINERARY FOUR
CANADIAN OPERATIONS/JUNO BEACH

JUNO BEACH LANDINGS - 3rd CANADIAN DIVISION

Assault Time:	0735 hours
Leading Formations:	6th Armoured Regiment (1st Hussars)
	DD tanks
	The Royal Winnipeg Rifles
	The Regina Rifle Regiment
	10th Armoured Regiment (Fort Garry Horse)
	DD Tanks
	The Queen's Own Rifles of Canada
	The North Shore (New Brunswick) Regiment
3rd Canadian Division Commander:	Major General R.F.L. Keller
Bombarding Force E:	Cruisers: HMS *Belfast* (flagship)
	HMS *Diadem*
	Eleven destroyers including the
	FFS *Combattante* (French)
German Defenders:	716th Infantry Division
716th Division Commander:	Lieutenant General Wilhelm Richter

The Plan

The plan was to assault on a two-brigade front astride the mouth of the River Seulles, with the 7th Brigade Group landing at Courseulles on MIKE sector and 8th Brigade Group landing at Bernières on NAN sector. Each brigade had DD floating tank support from the 6th Armoured and 10th Armoured Regiments respectively, plus fire support from the 107mm mortars of the Cameron Highlanders of Ottawa. The 8th Brigade was to be closely followed by elements of the 4th Special Service Brigade charged with mopping up, making contact with 3rd British Division Commandos and taking the German radar station at Douvres-la-Délivrande.

The Canadians' objectives were the capture and clearance of the coastal villages and towns along JUNO BEACH, particularly Courseulles, St Aubin and Bernières. The Division had three objective lines, 'Yew', 'Elm' and 'Oak', which corresponded to three phases in their D-Day plan.

What Happened on D-Day

The crossing for the troops at sea was rough which delayed the assault. Despite considerable opposition from entrenched German positions relatively unaffected by preliminary bombardments, the Canadians got ashore shortly after 0800 helped by fire support from two Canadian destroyers, the *Algonquin* and the *Sioux*.

By the end of the day they were practically everywhere beyond 'Elm', their intermediate objective line. General Keller's men had made the greatest gains of all on D-Day, in some places seven miles inland. On their right they had made contact with the 50th Northumbrian Division at Creully, but on their left was a dangerous gap between themselves and the British 3rd Division on SWORD. Into that gap General Eric Marcks, Commanding the German LXXXIV Corps, ordered Major General Edgar Feuchtinger's 21st Panzer Division. Then, that evening, south of Caen, the leading elements of 12th Waffen-SS Hitler Jugend Panzer Division, released that afternoon by Adolf Hitler, began to arrive. It was a critical moment.

THE BATTLEFIELD TOUR

THE TOUR STARTS NEAR CARPIQUET AIRPORT, CAEN.
It covers the 3rd Canadian Division's actions on JUNO Beach and inland towards Caen.

* Planned duration without stops for refreshments or extra visits: 5 hours
* Total distance: 23 miles
Take the D14/D220 Carpiquet/Authie exit from the N13. Set your mileometer to zero.

• Carpiquet/0 miles/Lat & Long: 49.19441 -0.43816
The route that you will take is essentially that of the 12th SS as they attempted to push the Canadians back to the beaches. The struggle in the area JUNO – Carpiquet, came down to a contest between the Canadians and the fanatical young Nazis of the Waffen SS.
Continue to Authie on the D220.
On entering Authie there is a white JUNO Itinerary sign. These signs mark the Canadians' advance inland and details can be obtained at the JUNO Beach museum.
Continue to the memorial on the left opposite the Mairie.

• North Nova Scotia Highlanders Memorial, Authie/1 mile/5 minutes
This Memorial commemorates the Nova Scotia Highlanders who in fighting around the village on 7 June lost 84 men killed and 158 wounded or taken prisoner. The Sherbrooke Rifles had 60 dead. Beside it is a **NTL Totem** describing the Canadians' progress from JUNO Beach to Buron on 7 June. Here in Authie leading elements of the Highlanders were attacked by Colonel Kurt Meyer's fanatical 25th Panzer Grenadiers who pressed forward regardless of their losses.
Continue over the D126 on the D220 to the Mairie square in St Contest-Buron.

• North Nova Scotia Highlanders and Sherbrooke Fusiliers Memorials, Buron/1.8 miles/10 minutes
The D220 road, down which you have driven, was a main axis for the Canadian forces moving inland from JUNO. It leads directly to the high ground at Carpiquet Airport three

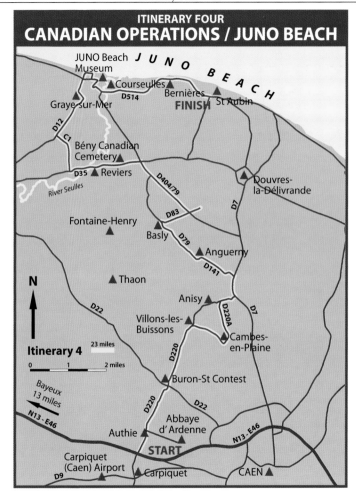

ITINERARY FOUR
CANADIAN OPERATIONS / JUNO BEACH

miles behind you. At the end of D-Day the Canadians had reached Villons-le-Buissons, 3½ miles north of here (ahead of you), and by around 0700 hours on 7 June the 9th Brigade, led by the North Nova Scotia Highlanders and the 27th Armoured Regiment (Sherbrooke Fusiliers), was advancing towards Buron which they took after a house to house battle.

At 1500 hours Meyer launched a counter-attack on Buron, hoping to drive to the sea in conjunction with 21st Panzer Division. Late in the afternoon the Canadians lost Buron and fell back to Villons-les-Buissons where they had begun the day. It had been a bloody struggle. The Highlanders had some 250 casualties and the Sherbrookes lost 21 cruiser tanks.

The battle for the high ground of Carpiquet was to be a long and hard one against fanatical troops of the 12th SS Panzer Division. The bulk of the soldiers were youngsters under 18 years old straight out of military fitness camps and full of Nazi ideology. In all, the division, which was initially commanded by *Brigadeführer* Fritz Witt, had about 20,000 men and 150 tanks.

On 8 July once again the 9th Brigade advanced on Buron. The Highland Light Infantry of Canada and the Sherbrookes led off at 0730 hours and by 0830 hours were in the village. The 12th SS Panzer Division, now commanded by Kurt Meyer following Fritz Witt's death on 14 June, held on until early the following morning. The Highland Light Infantry lost half of its attacking force in what had been its first real battle and it was to prove its bloodiest of the campaign with 262 casualties.

Here are Memorials to the Highland Light Infantry and to the Sherbrooke Fusiliers.

Continue on the D220 over the D22 crossroads and head north towards Villons-les-Buissons. At the first road junction left, just short of the village, stop.

• *Hell's Corner/9th Canadian Infantry Memorial, Villons-les-Buissons/3.0 miles/5 minutes*

Here is the Memorial to the 9th Canadian Infantry (Highland) Brigade that fought so determinedly between here and Buron from 6 June to 8 July. It was dedicated on 8 June 1984.

Continue to the Villons-les-Buissons village sign. Stop on the left.

• *B-16 Airstrip Memorial, Villons-les-Buissons/3.4 miles/5 minutes*

This commemorates the British and Norwegian units of the **84th Group 2nd TAF** who were based here.

Continue into the village along the Rue des Sherbrooke Fusiliers and take the first turning right on rue des Cambes along the château wall towards the junction with the D79. Stop on the left just before the junction.

• *Norwegian Memorial, Villons-les-Buissons/4.1 miles/5 minutes*

This Memorial is dedicated to the memory of the Norwegian fighters from 1940 to 1945. The only Allied naval casualty from attacks by German naval forces on D-Day was the Royal Norwegian Navy destroyer *Svenner* which had originally been HMS *Shark*. Launched in 1943 she had been transferred to the Norwegian Navy.

Continue straight over the junction into Cambes-en-Plaine bearing left to the church.
On the left is

• 59th (Staffs) Division, 3rd BR Division & 2nd Bn R Ulster Rifles Memorial, Cambes-en-Plaine/4.9 miles/10 minutes/Map H33a/Lat & Long: 49.23302 -0.38469

Both Divisions entered Caen on the afternoon of 9 July from the north as the 3rd Can Division simultaneously entered from the west. The large white Memorial bears the Plaques of the Divisions and the Regiment and the words 'Cambes-en-Plaine à ses Libérateurs'.

Continue to the junction and turn right to the cemetery.

• Cambes-en-Plaine CWGC Cemetery/5.2 miles/15 minutes

This unusual cemetery has a 'modern' yellow Caen stone entrance. More than half the 224 burials in this cemetery are of the North and South Staffordshire Regiments from the fighting of 8 and 9 July. Many of the personal inscriptions here are almost unbearably moving in their simple expressions of close family grief. The 6th North Staffords had passed through this area on 9 July having had 190 casualties (a quarter of their strength) in their first two days in action.

Continue to the small crossroads. On the right at the corner is

• 2nd Battalion Royal Ulster Rifles Memorial/5.2 miles/5 minutes

The Battalion captured the village of Cambes-en-Plaine on 9 June. Cambes was one of the strongest German positions on this part of the front and had repulsed a Canadian 9th Brigade attack on 7 June. The successful attack two days later was made in conjunction with the East Riding Yeomanry and reinforced by the King's Own Scottish Borderers. The taking of Cambes secured the junction between the Canadian (JUNO) and British (SWORD) forces.

The road here is called Rue du Lieutenant Lynn 8 juillet 1944.

Turn left up the small road and at the crossroads turn right signed Mathieu D220. After 200 yards stop at the memorial on the left.

• Queen's Own Rifles of Canada Memorial, Anisy/6.4 miles/5 minutes

The stone Memorial, with a cut-out maple leaf in the centre, remembers the members of the regiment who gave their lives to take and hold Anisy, their D-Day objective. It was unveiled on 6 June 1994.

Continue to the roundabout and turn left signed Anguerny. At the junction go straight over on the D141 and continue into the village. Just before the junction by the Church stop on the right. At the right hand corner is a

• Plaque Rond Point du Regt Fort Garry Horse 1944/Plaque to the Queen's Own Rifles of Canada, Anguerny/8.3 miles/5 minutes

The Fort Garry Horse Plaque was unveiled on 5 June 1994 and the Queen's Own is on the wall opposite.

Turn left on Rue Queen's Own Rifles of Canada and continue past the church to the junction with the D141/D141A. Stop by the Mairie. On the left hand corner is

9th Can Bde Memorial, Hell's Corner, Villons-les-Buissons.

North Nova Scotia Highlanders Memorial, Authie.

The unusual entrance to Cambes-en-Plaine CWGC Cemetery.

Regt Fort Garry Horse Memorial, Anguerny.

• Memorial to the Régiment de la Chaudière, Anguerny's Liberators/8.4 miles/5 minutes

The black marble Plaque lists seven members of the regiment who died on 6 and 8 June 1944.

Turn right direction Basly on the D141A on rue Régiment de la Chaudière, 6 juin 1944. Continue to the junction with the D79 and turn right. Continue into the village and stop at the memorial by the Church.

• Maple Leaf Memorial, Basly/9.8 miles/5 minutes

This was erected on 8 June 1991 by the citizens of Basly in gratitude to their Canadian liberators.

Continue on the D79 and turn right at the T junction then bear left on the D83 direction Douvres. Cross the D404 and stop at the museum on the left.

• Douvres Radar Station Museum/10.9 miles/20 minutes/Lat & Long: 49.28572 -0.40307

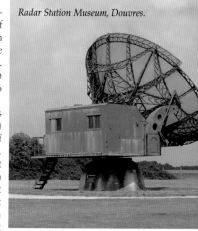

Radar Station Museum, Douvres.

The Museum is housed in two remarkably well-preserved bunkers and charts the evolution of radar (Radio Aid to Detection And Ranging). In front of it is a **NTL Totem** and to the left is a white **MLC Marker** and beyond a **Wurzburg Antenna**. **Open:** 1 July-31 August (though these times can vary). Entrance fee payable. Tel: +(0)2 31 06 06 45.

The task of taking the radar station was allocated to the North Shore (New Brunswick) Regiment. It had reached the village of Tailleville, barely a mile north (ahead) of here, on the night of 6 June but when it moved off at 0700 hours on 7 June it met heavy opposition in the woods on the far side of the field to the left (north) and the task was passed to the 51st Highland Division. That evening the 5th Battalion Black Watch attacked the station but made no impression, though unfortunately it seems that the Black Watch and the New Brunswicks may have briefly fought each other.

The station position, stretched along the 50-metre contour line, is

Canadian CWGC Cemetery, Bény-sur-Mer.

plumb in the middle of the 6th/7th June gap that existed between the British and Canadian armies. At 1500 hours on 6 June, 21st Panzer Division was advancing into that gap east of Douvres. The British 3rd Division stayed the bulk of 21st Panzer but a small force of infantry and tanks reached Luc-sur-Mer. The Canadians steeled themselves for a major assault but the follow-up armada of 250 gliders for 6AB Division arriving at 2100 hours gave the Germans the impression that they would be surrounded, and by the time that they had figured out where they had landed it was too dark to attack.

The radar station proved to be so difficult that General Dempsey decided to bypass it. Eventually a combat group of 22nd Dragoons, No 41 RM Commando and 26th Assault Squadron RE attacked uphill towards you from the village of Douvres ahead (with its twin church spires). Flail tanks led the way through the minefield followed by AVREs. Heavy artillery gave covering fire. High explosive charges were laid against the blockhouses and the Commandos went in under cover of smoke. It was a short, furious battle, and the Germans raised the white flag. But it was 17 June, almost 2 weeks after D-Day.

Return to the D404 and turn right. After 1.5 miles on the right is the small

• Memorial to RCAF ALG B4/12.6 miles/5 minutes
The strip, 1200 metres long, was completed on 15 June.
  Continue to the roundabout and turn left onto the D35.

• Canadian CWGC Cemetery, Cameron Highlanders of Ottawa Memorial/Bény-sur-Mer/13.7 miles/20 minutes/Lat & Long: 49.30230 -0.45067

This is the highest point for some miles around and there are two watch-towers from which excellent views may be obtained towards Courseulles and JUNO Beach. At the bottom of the left-hand tower is a **Memorial Tablet** to the **Cameron Highlanders of Ottawa**. There are 2,049 graves in the cemetery, 2,044 of which are Canadian, including 335 officers and men of the 3rd Canadian Division who were killed on D-Day. Among them are nine pairs of brothers - **Blais, Boyd, Branton, Hadden, Hobbin, Mekin, Skwarchuk, Tadgell and White**. There are three **Westlake** brothers - Rifleman T.L. of the Queen's Own Rifles of Canada, age 33 and Rifleman A.N., age 26 of the same regiment, both killed on 11 June and buried side by side in Plot III Row D and **Private George**, of the Nova Scotia Highlanders, killed on 7 June who is in Plot VIII Row F12. Also buried here is **Lieutenant Edward Frank Mantle** of the 5th Anti-Tank Regiment, RCA, killed on 2 August. His father, **Major Alfred Mantle**, was killed in the First World War on 26 September 1916 and is commemorated on the Vimy Memorial.

Continue towards the village of Reviers and as the road enters the village there is a road junction to the left with a small memorial.

• Regina Rifle Regiment Memorial, Reviers/14.3 miles/5 minutes
The small plaque and stone are to the Regina Rifle Regiment who liberated Reviers on D-Day. They and their fellow regiment of the 7th Brigade, the Royal Winnipeg Rifles, moved rapidly off the beach at Courseulles and by mid-morning were two miles inland,

completing their task of seizing the crossings over the River Seulles which lie at the bottom of this hill.

> Continue on the D176/35 following signs to Bayeux and immediately after crossing the River Seulles turn right towards Banville on the C1. In the village turn right onto the D12 signed Courseulles and at Graye-sur-Mer turn left just before the river. Follow signs to Centre Ville and Croix de Lorraine. (Do not take to the road to Courseulles). Turn right at the War Memorial following the Croix de Lorraine sign. Continue on the D112C to, on the left,

• Plaques to the Royal Winnipeg Rifles/Canadian Scottish/18.1 miles/5 minutes/Lat & Long: 49.33355 -0.47150

Two bronze **Plaques** were unveiled on this renovated *lavoir* on 5 June 1994 (D-Day + 50 Years) to commemorate Graye's liberation by these regiments, whose badges are on the Memorial.

> Continue to the junction with the D514 coast road and go straight across towards the beach and a tank in the dunes, signed la Brèche de Graye/Croix de Lorraine along Avénue Général de Gaulle.

On the corner on the left is a **sign listing the VIPs who landed here**, including Gen Montgomery (8 June), Winston Churchill and Gen Smuts (12 June), Gen de Gaulle (14 June) and King George V1 (on 16 June).

• Graye Churchill Tank/Comité du Débarquement Monument /Cross of Lorraine/R Winnipeg Rifles & Can Scottish Memorial, XXIInd Dragoons Plaque/18.4 miles/15 minutes

By the *Comité du Débarquement* Signal Monument is a Churchill tank AVRE with a petard. Both are at the junction of the Green (left) and Red (right) sectors of Mike/JUNO Beach where the Royal Winnipeg Rifles came ashore together with elements of the 6th Canadian Armoured Regiment. They were to suffer 128 casualties, the second heaviest Canadian regimental casualties of the day. Accompanying the Canadians were the 1st and 2nd Troops of the 26th Assault Squadron Royal Engineers charged with clearing exits off the beach through the obstacles and the dunes. The leading AVRE touched down about 0755 hours, somewhat behind the DD tanks and assault infantry. At this exit there was an anti-tank ditch and just south of it a flooded culvert connected to the River Seulles.

This tank, commanded by Bill Dunn, slid down into the flooded culvert. Water poured into the tank, so the crew scrambled out and, escorted by another tank, made their way back to the dunes, where they lay down behind a sandbank. There they were hit by mortar bombs and Sappers Manley, Philips and Batson were killed. Manley is buried in the Bayeux CWGC Cemetery but there seem to be no records for the other two. That afternoon the two survivors, Bill Dunn and Bill Hawkins, were evacuated to England. Six days later Winston Churchill landed here, followed by HM King George V1 on 16 June.

The sunken tank was incorporated into the exit road and there it stayed until 1976 when it was recovered. The ceremony inaugurating the tank as a memorial was attended by both survivors. At the edge of the car park is a granite **Memorial** with a red Maple Leaf to the **Royal Winnipeg Rifles and Canadian Scottish** who suffered heavy losses at Graye-sur-Mer. In the dunes above is a large metal **Cross of Lorraine**, below which is a **NTL Totem**. At the bottom of the path leading to the Cross is a small **Plaque to the XXIInd Dragoons Flail Tanks** who landed on this beach on 6 June 1944 to clear minefields.

From the car park by the tank, continue on the road past the Cross of Lorraine towards JUNO Beach Centre, passing on the left

'Cosy' **Bunker**, tilting heavily into the sand. It was the site of intense fighting on D-Day and owes its name to **Lt William F. ("Cosy") Aitken** of B Coy R Winnipeg Rifles. His No 10 Platoon stormed the bunker with machine-gun and rifle fire and captured it by hurling grenades through the apertures. Lt Aitken was hit in the lungs during the fighting but returned to action after 3½ months in hospital. On 6 June 2004 a commemorative **Plaque** was unveiled on the bunker (which talks of 'Sgt' Cosy). There is also a bench with a photo and the story of **Sgt Leo Gariépy** (qv) of the 1st Hussars. These are part of the JUNO Park Tour (see below).

Continue to the parking for the Centre.

• JUNO Beach Centre & Memorials/18.7 miles/45 minutes/WC/Lat & Long: 49.33618 -0.46099

Inaugurated on 6 June 2003 by the Prime Ministers of Canada and France, the Centre, is 'a place to remember, a place to learn and a place of culture'. Donors can fund 'bricks' to pay tribute to individual WW2 Veterans. They are then mounted on blue 'Donor Kiosks' outside the Museum. By the car park is an **NTL Totem**. In the courtyard is a dramatic **sculpture** entitled '**Remembrance and Renewal**' by Colin Gibson. It depicts five stylised military figures in a circle looking outwards expressing various qualities such as leadership, vigour and alertness, sombre reflection and the help of comrades.

On 30 October 2005 a 'windows-style messenger'

'Donor Kiosks', JUNO Beach Centre.

Inuksuk Monument, JUNO Beach Centre.

Inuksuk Monument (which acts as a telescope inviting the visitor to look at a distant point of significance) was inaugurated to the right of the entrance. It was built by Inuk Elder Peter Irniq who described the window as connecting the graves of fallen warriors resting in Europe with their loved ones in Canada and vice-versa.

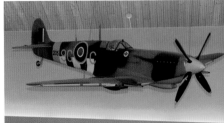

Model 443 Sqn Mk IX Spitfire, JUNO Beach Centre.

Inside are 5 rooms devoted to Canada prior to and during WW2; Canada in the '30s; Canada goes to war; Courseulles 6 June 1944; Canadian campaigns in Europe up to VE Day; personal stories of Canadians of the period – they are extremely moving audio-visual presentations. Two rooms are devoted to Canada today and to the Inuit.

There is a storyline for children to follow through the eyes of young Canadians Peter and Madeleine and imaginative new programmes for young people (tailored to ages 7-12 and 13-18) using Canadian guides assuming the role of nurses or soldiers, hands-on displays of uniforms and artefacts, urban warfare, quizzes, interactive stations, films and games. There is a documentation room with Internet access and reference works and an attractive book, map, gift and souvenir shop and wheelchair access.

A visit to the Centre is highly recommended. There is a welcoming atmosphere to this museum, in large part engendered by the enthusiastic young Canadian guides, who speak of the privilege they feel to serve here, and the dedicated Director, Nathalie Worthington.

In September 2004 the JUNO Park, which surrounds the Museum and which was largely funded by the Commune of Courseulles, was inaugurated. Dotted throughout it are groups of Information Panels with photographs/newspaper accounts/veterans' personal memories etc. and the Museum provides a unique, daily 45 mins, 2km **Beach Tour'** at 1000, 1100, 1200, 1300, 1400 and 1500 in June, July, August in English/French (3 in each language) and at 1100 and 1500 in April, May, September and October.

Sherman tank with, behind, Gen de Gaulle Mem, Courseulles.

Open: daily 1 April – 30 September 0930-1900. March and October1000-1800. Feb, Nov, Dec: 1000-1300 and 1400-1700. **Closed** January and Christmas Day. Entrance fee payable. Tel: +(0)2 31 37 32 17. Fax: +(0)2 31 37 83 69. E-mail: contact@junobeach.org Website: www.junobeach.org

> *Return towards the Cross of Lorraine and turn left over the small bridge opposite the Ecole de Voile.*

At the far end of the bridge on the right is a **Plaque to Nottingham Bridge**. It was erected in 1994 by the **85th Field Coy RE** and the Plaque was placed to commemorate the 50th anniversary of D-Day by 'Old comrades of 85th Fld Coy, RE, who landed at Graye-sur-Mer in the early hours of D-Day 6 June 1944'. It has a handsome frame with badges in *bas relief* and was named after Lt-Col F.C. Nottingham. (**Lat & Long: 49.33595 -0.46497**).

> *Continue to the T junction, turn left and turn right just before the swing bridge following the one way system.*

On the Quai des Alliés is the attractive ** Logis de France, **Hotel-Restaurant Belle Aurore**. 7 en-suite rooms. Local fish and seafood specialitiesTel: + (0)2 31 37 46 23

> *Drive completely around the harbour towards the Maison de la Mer. Three hundred yards later stop near a Sherman tank in Place Général de Gaulle.*

• *Courseulles Memorials/19.7 miles/20 minutes/Lat & Long: 49.33608 - 0.45748*

This seaside town where the River Seulles reaches the sea was the aiming point for the 7th Canadian Infantry Brigade Group. Its task was to clear Courseulles and move rapidly inland to gain the crossings over the River Seulles. In a leap-frogging operation, including the use of the 9th Brigade, the follow-up force, the Canadians' target was the high ground around Carpiquet just south of the N13. The bad weather delayed the assault and most of the infantry landed ahead of the tanks. The delay in the arrival of the tanks might have been greater but for the initiative of some of the DD tank commanders, like Sergeant Leo Gariépy (qv) of B Squadron, who launched on their own initiative. Gariépy was probably the first to land.

The assault battalion here, east of the Seulles, was the Regina Rifles and A and B Companies hit the shore about 0800 hours. They were immediately fired upon from concrete strongpoints. The following companies lost many men as their assault craft hit mined obstacles some 200 yards out to sea and the Canadians had a hard struggle to get ashore. Nevertheless, the Reginas, helped by the tanks of the 1st Hussars, (6th Canadian Armoured Regiment), forced their way through and around the town.

In 1970 a **Canadian Sherman DD** was recovered from the sea and Leo Gariépy helped to raise money to place it here. Gariépy was present, although sadly he died a year later. On the side of the tank is a row of regimental plaques and the following Memorials are around the square:

NTL Totem
A Plaque describing the action on JUNO Beach.
German anti-tank gun KWK 39 used on 6 June 1944 and restored in 1994.
A Memorial commemorating de Gaulle's landing here on 14 June.
A Memorial on one side of the beach entrance erected on 6 June 1969 with **Plaques** to

the **1st Canadian Scottish Regiment, Belgian Volunteers, the 8th Bn the R Scots, the 6th Bn R Scots Fus and the 6th Border Bn King's Own Scottish Borderers** who landed near this spot June 1944 as 44th Lowland Bde.

A Plaque on the other side of the beach entrance to the **458 officers and men of the Regina Regiment** who fell from 1939 to 1945.

A Memorial to the French destroyer *la Combattante*. She was part of the supporting Bombardment Group and was built in 1942 at the Fairfields Yard in Glasgow. Her original name was HMS *Haldon* and she was loaned to the Free French Navy. On 23 February 1945 she was torpedoed east of Dungeness by the German Midget Submarine U5330. Sixty-five French and two Royal Navy sailors were lost.

Over the road in Place du 6 Juin is the ** **Hotel de Paris**. 27 comfortable rooms, some with sea view. Pleasant restaurant, bar and terrace. Fish and seafood specialities. Variety of menus and *à la carte*. Tel: + +(0)2 31 37 45 07 . E-mail: hoteldeparis-normandie@wanadoo.fr **Closed** 13/11-31/01.

Walk some 200 yards to the east along the promenade to

'Little Black Devils', the Royal Winnipeg Rifles Memorial which is a huge memorial dagger, erected on 6 June 1964. On the seafront side is a coloured regimental badge. Beside it is **La Crémaillère Restaurant** with superb cuisine, lovely sea view and warm welcome. Its hotel, 100 metres away, Logis de France **Le Gytan**, has 43 rooms. Tel: +(0)2 31 37 46 73. E-mail: cremaillere@wanadoo.fr

Continue along the Avénue de la Combattante and then on the D514 following signs to Bernières and Ouistreham. As the road returns to the coast on entering Bernières there is a large clearing, Place du 6 juin, on the left with a Comité du Débarquement Monument. Stop.

This was the first of these monuments erected along the Normandy landing beaches to commemorate 'Le Jour J'. The foundation stone was laid on 6 June 1949.

• Comité du Débarquement Monument/Bunker and Memorials /First Journalists Plaque, Bernières /21.8 miles/20 minutes

This was the centre of the assault area of the 8th Canadian Brigade Group and the sector here is NAN White. The assault regiment was the Queen's Own Rifles of Canada and they had the largest D-Day casualties of any Canadian unit. The Germans had constructed a 'Wiederstandsnester', a resistance nest, with mutually supporting weapons and good fields of fire using concrete bunkers and connecting trenches.

The Queen's Own landed at about 0815 hours without tank support (it was too rough to launch the DDs), and some 200 yards east of its target - right in front of the *Wiederstandsnester*. The leading company lost half its strength running over the beach to the sea wall, but, thanks to the support of a flak ship the Germans were so effectively silenced that only snipers were active when the Régiment de la Chaudière began to land fifteen minutes later. The Canadians headed inland towards the D79 leading to Bény, but German 88mm guns and machine guns stopped the advance. The divisional commander, not aware of the hold-up inland, ordered the follow-up brigade, the 9th, to land and by midday the whole area was packed solid. It was one huge traffic jam and the 9th could not get moving until around 1600 hours. Without the jam the 9th might have reached

Carpiquet that night before the 12th SS, and the battle for Caen *might* have been quite different.

On the beach here a sapper bulldozer driver silenced one pillbox by driving up behind it and filling it with sand.

In the square is the welcoming **Restaurant-Crêperie L'Estran**. You will find a tasty lunch here when many other restaurants have closed. Excellent *galettes*. Tel: +(0)2 31 37 19 48. **Closed** 2 weeks in Dec and Jan. **Closed** Mon except July/Aug.

From the Comité Monument walk 250 yards to the east along the promenade to the large bunker.

German Bunker. Lat & Long: 49.33568 -0.41957. There is a NTL Totem at the entrance to the draw. It is in an area called Place du Canada and on and beside it are **Memorials** to the **Queen's Own Rifles** of Canada and **Le Régiment de la Chaudière**. There is a bronze

Plaque to **8th Brigade** 3rd Canadian Infantry Division. A **Plaque** headed 'In Peace Paratus' bears the lines, 'Stand for a moment and imagine what it must have been like when 800 men of the **Queen's Own Rifles** of **Canada** stormed ashore at this very spot on 6 June 1944. We will remember them!' There is a **Plaque** to the **5th Hackney Battalion** the Royal Berks Regiment and **No 8 Beach Group** who landed here with the assault troops and a **Memorial** to the **Fort Garry Horse** 10th Armoured Regiment

'Canadian' Bunker, Bernières.

unveiled in 1994. On a separate bunker is a **Plaque** to the **Régiment de la Chaudière** erected by the *Commission des Monuments Historiques de Québec*. A bronze **Plaque** erected in 1999 by the Historic Sites and Monuments Board of Canada has a marvellous *bas relief* map of the Canadian landings and progress, 6-9 June 1944. There is also a *Plaque* to the **Stormont Dundas & Glengarry Highlanders**.

Return to Place du 6 Juin. Walk over the D514 to the road leading straight ahead.

The press had established themselves in the centre of Bernières even earlier - at 1030 hours - in the Hotel de Grave, now a private house, No. 288, the first on the left in the Rue du Régiment de la Chaudière. There is a **Plaque** there to commemorate '**The first HQ for journalists**, photographers and moviemakers, British and Canadian from which the first reports destined for the press and the radio of the world were despatched.' To its right is a *bas relief* bronze showing details of **the Canadian Landings**. One thing in particular surprised the local inhabitants. The 'Tommies' spoke French.

Just past the **Office de Tourisme** (and WC, into which the bus shelter gives uninterrupted views) is a striking symbolic male statue formed from large chunks of stone commemorating the **Inuit** Canadians, inaugurated on 6 June 2004.

Continue on the D514 to St Aubin Plage keeping to the sea front and stop by the German bunker.

• Fort Garry Horse, North Shore, No 48 RM Commando, Maurice Duclos Memorials, Bunker, St Aubin/23.2 miles/10 minutes/Lat & Long: 49.33254 -0.39492

The area to the east of here has no suitable beach for a major landing until la Brêche d'Hermanville on GOLD is reached some four miles away, therefore special forces such as commandos went ashore, one of whose tasks was to fill the gaps between the main landings. No 48 RM Commando were to land here at St Aubin and to move east, while No 41 RM Commando were to land at Lion-sur-Mer and move this way. They were supposed to meet at Petit Enfer two miles east of here, which was a German strongpoint.

The North Shore Regiment of Canada who landed here overcame the German strongpoints using their DD tanks, and AVREs. The 50mm gun in the bunker put out of action some of the leading tanks but was eventually silenced by two tanks and a RM Centaur. About four hours after landing the beach was clear except for one strongpoint and a number of snipers and the Commandos struck out to Langrune.

There is a **NTL Totem** here which describes the charge of No 48 Commando over the rocks. To the left of the bunker are **Memorials** to the **Fort Garry Horse, 5 Field Company RCE, 19 Field Regiment RCA; North Shore Regiment, No 48 RM Commando, civilian victims and to Maurice Duclos**, a French secret agent code-named 'Saint Jacques' who landed here on 4 August 1940.

One hundred yards to the right of the bunker, in front of the **Syndicat d'Initiative** (**Tourist Office**, Tel: +(0)2 31 97 30 41, E-mail: otstaubin@orange.fr) is a stone **Memorial** to the **10th Canadian Armoured Regiment, Fort Garry Horse**, erected in 1965.

End of Itinerary 4

Memorials Area, St Aubin.

ITINERARY FIVE
ALLIED COMMANDO OPS/SWORD BEACH

SWORD BEACH LANDINGS - 3rd BRITISH DIVISION

Assault Time:	0725 hours
Leading Formations:	8th Infantry Brigade Group
	13th/18th Hussars DD Tanks
	1st South Lancashire Regiment
	2nd East Yorkshire Regiment
3rd British Division Commander:	Major General T.G. Rennie
Bombarding Force D:	Battleships: HMS *Warspite*
	HMS *Ramillies*
	Monitor: HMS *Roberts*
	Cruisers: HMS *Mauritius* (flagship)
	HMS *Arethusa*
	HMS *Frobisher*
	HMS *Danal*
	ORP *Dragon* (Polish)
	13 destroyers including HNMS *Svenner* (Norwegian)
German Defenders:	716th Infantry Division

The 3rd British Division had last been in action at Dunkirk, and most of its soldiers had since then only served on the Home Front. Because of the variation in the time of the tides between UTAH and SWORD, the landing here came one hour after the Americans and ninety minutes after dawn. Therefore the Germans were both alert to a seaborne assault and able to see the landing craft coming in.

The Plan - SWORD Beach Landing

In formulating his plan for 1st British Corps, Lieutenant General Crocker was acutely aware that the 21st Panzer Division was in or around Caen. His eastern flank was well defined by the Orne river and canal and they were to be secured by the Special Service Brigade, plus 6th Airborne Division, but if the 21st Panzer Division reacted quickly and 12th SS Panzer joined them, he would be much inferior in armoured strength and likely to be thrown back into the sea. Thus it was important that the extreme eastern division, the 3rd British Division, should break through the defence crust and move rapidly inland in anticipation of an armoured counter-attack.

The plan of the 3rd British Division Commander, Major General T.G. Rennie, was to attack on a single brigade front on White and Red sectors of QUEEN Beach. The 8th Infantry Brigade Group, the first to land, had a number of tasks: to secure the landing areas; to relieve 6th Airborne Division at Pegasus Bridge; No 4 Commando to clear east to Ouistreham; No 41 Royal Marine Commando to clear west to the Canadians at Langrune; and 1st Special Service Brigade to move east across Pegasus Bridge. Following up was the 185th Infantry Brigade Group. Their task was to pass through 8th Brigade and to 'seize Caen' - the most ambitious aim of all.

What Happened on D-Day - SWORD Beach Landings

Naval Force S for SWORD gathered off the beach in the early hours of 6 June. Just before daylight a smoke screen was laid by aircraft between the ships and the coastal batteries at le Havre. In the morning gloom, thickened with smoke, four German E-Boats appeared, fired torpedoes and vanished. The *Warspite* and the *Ramillies* had narrow misses but the Norwegian destroyer *Svenner* was hit and sank. That was all that Admiral Ramsay's invasion fleet saw of the German Navy on D-Day.

The bombardment followed the pattern employed everywhere else, though SWORD probably had the most intensive attention of all of the beaches, and it was concentrated on a strip 3 miles long and $\frac{1}{2}$ mile deep.

Despite the rough seas, the DD tanks of the 13th/18th Hussars and the LCT-borne 'Funnies' of the Engineer Assault Teams hit the beaches ahead of the LCAs of the infantry. Of the twenty-five tanks launched, twenty-one made the shore and these, together with the flail tanks of 22nd Royal Dragoons, gave immediate fire support to the infantry battalions.

The South Lancashire and East Yorkshire Regiments were off the beaches within an hour, though stubborn German resistance continued in la Brêche, the centre of the landing beach, until around 1030 hours. The 185th Infantry Brigade began coming ashore mid-morning and passed through the 8th Brigade, but enemy resistance on the Periers Ridge, between Douvres and Bénouville, on which the Radar Station and the Hillman Bunker sat, prevented rapid movement inland.

By the end of the day the 2nd Battalion King's Shropshire Light Infantry, part of 185th Brigade, whose task it had been to ride on the tanks of the Staffordshire Yeomanry into Caen on 6 June, were still four miles short. Another forty-three days would pass before Caen fell.

THE TOUR STARTS IN LANGRUNE.

It can be taken immediately after the end of Itinerary 4.

* Planned duration without stops for refreshments or extra visits: 3 hours 30 minutes
* Total distance: 14.4 miles

To reach Langrune from the E46 Caen ring road take the Hérouville-St-Clair exit and follow signs on the D7. Stop near the Tourist Office. **Set your mileometer to zero.**
TOURIST OFFICE. Tel: +(0)2 31 97 32 77. E-mail: tourisme.langrune-sur-mer@wanadoo.fr

• No 48 RM Commando/Work of War Memorials, Langrune/0 miles/10 minutes/Lat & Long: 49.32537 -0.36998

This seafront road and the parallel one behind it had been strongly fortified by the

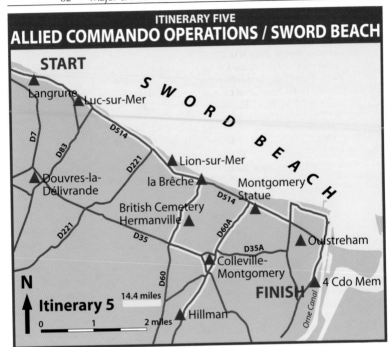

ITINERARY FIVE
ALLIED COMMANDO OPERATIONS / SWORD BEACH

Germans. Coming in on the parallel road from St Aubin, the Commandos enlisted the help of a naval bombardment and a Centaur tank of the 5 (Independent) RM Armd Spt Bty to help them break through to the seafront. Further efforts involved an anti-tank gun and a Sherman tank, which was immobilised. It was a bitter hand-to-hand battle, which was not won until late on 7 June, when thirty-one German prisoners were taken, but the Commandos had over 100 casualties. The **Memorial Stone** commemorates **No 48 RM Commando** on one side and on the other, under the coat of arms of Langrune and the *Croix de Guerre*, the command,

*48 RM Cdo
Memorial, Langrune.*

Souviens-toi! (Remember!). In front and to the left of the memorial is a dramatic cubic sculpture made out of compacted debris of war with the caption, 'This is a not a work of arts. This is a work of war 1944-1994. Never again.' It was presented by the sculptor, Dominique Colas. Beside it is a **NTL Totem** to Langrune Fortified Town.

Continue on the D514 to Luc-sur-Mer. Pass the Casino and **Tourist Office**. Tel: (0)2 31 97 33 25. E-mail: luc.sur.mer@wanadoo.fr *and stop at the eastern end of the sea front near the* Hotel-Restaurant **Le Beau Rivage** (renovated Logis de France. 20 rooms. Tel: +(0)2 31 96 49 51. E-mail: mlefevre24@club-internet.fr) *in Square Capitaine Tom Gordon Hemming.*

• *First Commando Raid, 1941/Liberation/Capt T.G. Hemming Memorials, Luc-sur-Mer/Petit Enfer/1.0 mile/10 minutes*

This is the boundary between JUNO and SWORD Beaches, the town itself being in SWORD. It was to here that the small detachment of 21st Panzer advanced on the evening of 6 June to find the German defences intact, and it was the arrival of 6th AB Division's follow-up glider force that so stunned 21st Panzer's commanding general that by the time he recovered it was too dark to reinforce the advance. By the following day it was too late.

The **Memorial** asks the passer-by to remember '*le premier commando allié en Normandie, 28 Septembre 1941*' - the first allied commando raid on Normandy 28 September 1941. At the foot of the **Memorial is a Plaque to 'Capitaine Tom Gordon-Hemming**'. The reference to Captain Hemming is a mystery because it does not seem that he was on the raid. He was certainly part of No 2 Commando employed during the Salerno landings in 1943 when 4th Troop, which Hemming commanded, took 35

RM Cdo 'Sundial', NTL totem and ...urchill tank in the background, ...n-sur-Mer.

Memorials area, la Brèche d'Hermanville.

prisoners. The raid referred to here was carried out on the night of 27 September 1941 by 5th Troop of No 1 Commando. Their intended landing place had been Courseulles but as they approached the shore their commander, Captain Davies, realised that they were heading for St Aubin and decided to go ahead anyway. As they landed, a machine gun fired at them and Davies led an assault over the sea wall. Two more machine guns joined in and the commandos had to withdraw. Two commandos were missing and one was wounded. However, there is some confusion about where this took place and whether a German bicycle patrol had been involved. Whatever the truth, the Memorial is here. It also commemorates the liberation of Luc on 6/7 June 1944.

Continue on the D514 to Lion-sur-Mer. At the roundabout at the entrance to the town stop in the car park to the left. Walk back to the tank and memorials.

• Churchill Tank, No 41 RM Commando Sundial Memorial, Roosevelt Quotes Plaque/41 RM Commando Plaque, Lion-sur-Mer/2.6 miles/10 minutes/Lat & Long: 49.305934 -0.324489

No 41 RM Commando landed here, having crossed the Channel in 'LCI(S)' - Landing Craft Infantry (Small). At about 0845 hours they hit the sand some 200 yards out under intense mortar and shell fire and not exactly on target. Lieutenant-Colonel T.M. Gray, CO of No 41 RM Commando, sent part of his force to the east to make contact with the South Lancashire Regiment and part into the town. Between 1600 hours and 1800 hours destroyers fired upon German positions in the town, but the defenders were still there the following morning. A set-piece attack by the 5th Lincolnshires supported by the Royal Ulster Rifles and No 41 Commando enabled the Commandos to move on that evening to Luc-sur-Mer to join up with No 46 Commando.

There is a **NTL Totem** here and the spectacular **Memorial to No 41 RM Commando** is a symbolic sundial. The **Churchill Tank** was offered by General Sir Ian Harris who commanded 2nd Battalion The Royal Ulster Rifles. There is also a **Plaque to 41 RM Commando** with a Roll of Honour of 30 names, and a **Plaque with a Pres Roosevelt quote**.

Continue through the town on the D514 and take the second turning left after the traffic lights (Rue Marotte) and at the next junction turn left and stop immediately by the car park on the right.

• Place du No 41 Commando/Libération and Royal Engineer Memorials, Lion-sur-Mer/3.3 miles/10 minutes

The square has been named after the Commandos who landed here. The headstone-like stone nearby indicating Kiebingen 871 kms refers to town twinning.

Walk to the Promenade and turn left. Continue some 200 yards, passing the Lion War Memorial.

The **Monument** was unveiled by General Sir George Cooper GCB MC on the occasion of the granting of the freedom of Lion-sur-Mer to the **Corps of Royal Engineers** on 10 June 1989 to commemorate the part played by **77th Assault Squadron RE** in the liberation of the town 6 June 1944 and the continued links.

Return to your car and continue to the junction with the D514 and turn left to

Hermanville-sur-Mer. On entering la Brêche fork left at the red British phone box and park as soon as you can.

• La Brêche d'Hermanville Memorials to 3rd Division, S Lancs Regiment, Royal Artillery Units/'Pionniers'/Gooseberry,/Plaques to 2nd/5th Yorks, 13th/18th R Hussars, Norwegian Matelot/Churchill AVRE/4.6 miles/15 minutes/Lat & Long: 49.29743 -0.30236

The upright Memorial acknowledges a number of formations on either side:

'**Pionniers alliés. Le 5 juin 2300 heures**'. Presumably this acknowledges the work of the two midget submarines X20 and X23 that marked the edges of the British beaches, though they were actually in position by 2300 hours on 4 June in anticipation of the original date for D-Day of 5 June. **3rd Division. 27th Tank Brigade. Royal Marine Commandos. 101st Beach Sub-Area**.

Ships making up the Gooseberry off SWORD Beach including the *Courbet* (she had been part of the fleet that sailed in the Gallipoli affair in 1915) the *Centurion*, the *Durban* and the *Sumatra*.

To the left is a **Memorial to the S Lancs** (Prince of Wales Volunteers) Regiment who lost 288 officers and men on D-Day and in the subsequent campaign. In the ground before the memorial is the triangular emblem of **3rd British Division** in red and black and to the right a **Royal Artillery Memorial** listing 7th Field Regiment (SP) RA, 33rd Field Regiment, 76th Highland Field Regiment and 92nd LAA Regiment RA. Behind is the bronze **Statue to 'Le Matelot'** de Per Palle Storm and the Norwegian Royal Marines who participated in Operation Neptune. Cast in Oslo in 1992 it was inaugurated here on 7 June 2004 by HM King Harald of Norway. Beyond the statue is the **anchor of the *Svenner*** (qv).

On the wall to the left are **Plaques to the 2nd/5th E. Yorks Regt** who landed in the first wave on 6 June 1944 and to the **13th/18th R Hussars** whose flail tanks cleared the minefields.

In the **Tourist Office** building there are often D-Day exhibitions during the season. Enquire at the **Mairie** (see below) Tel: +(0)2 31 97 20 15.

You are now approximately in the centre of SWORD Beach, on QUEEN sector. The beach stretches for about 1.5 miles in each direction. As you face out to sea to your left is QUEEN White. To the right is QUEEN Red. The assault infantry on QUEEN White was the 1st South Lancashire Regiment, and on Red the 2nd East Yorkshire Regiment. The sight that faced the defenders in the early light of 6 June 1944 must have been terrifying. The sea was full of ships, the sky alive with aeroplanes. In the gap between flew hundreds of barrage balloons, while, driving rapidly towards the shore, were landing craft carrying the infantry. In front of them were the DD floating tanks of the 13th/18th Hussars.

Twenty-one DDs made it ashore, and it was these tanks, and the other specialised armour of Major General Sir Percy Hobart's 79th Armoured Division, that enabled major exits to be cleared from Red and White sectors within 2 hours. There were no minefields on the beaches here, though the lateral and exit roads were heavily mined. Following the initial landings just after a low tide, the sea came in rapidly, hiding the obstacles and making their clearance difficult. The water pushed those troops ashore up against the promenade where you now are, and they suffered heavily from enemy machine-gun and small-arms fire, particular on Red from the 3 o'clock direction. Into this turmoil at 0820 hours came No 4 Commando, complete with Piper Bill Millin, playing *Highland Laddie*, and stormed their way past the German shoreline defences, re-organised, then moved off to Ouistreham, which can be seen along the beach to the right.

The only significant German air attack came from eight aircraft the following morning. One was shot down and crashed 300 yards away to the right from the beach exit. Slightly right of centre, 1,100 yards out to sea, was the wreck of the French Cruiser, the *Courbet*, sunk as a Gooseberry blockship to provide protection for craft landing on SWORD Beach. There she proudly flew the *Tricolore* and the Cross of Lorraine, making her a favourite target for the Germans, ignorant of her helplessness. She was shelled, bombed and attacked by human torpedoes. German radio on 8 July claimed that their attacks had driven the *Courbet* ashore.

The order of landing of 8th Infantry Brigade Group from H-Hour at 0725 hours was:

1. A and B Squadrons of 13th/18th Hussars. DD tanks.
2. Eight Royal Engineer (77th and 79th Assault Squadrons) obstacle-gapping teams, each one made up of two flail tanks of 22nd Dragoons, three AVREs and one bulldozer.
3. Two obstacle-clearing teams, each of four flail tanks and four AVREs.
4. The assault infantry:
   QUEEN White - two companies of the 1st South Lancashire Regiment.
   QUEEN Red - two companies of the 2nd East Yorkshire Regiment.
5. At 0734 hours the HQ elements of the assault infantry plus their remaining two companies.
6. At 0810 hours HQ and C Squadron 13th/18th Hussars.
7. At 0825 hours the 1st Suffolk Regiment, the reserve battalion, plus 8th Brigade alternative main HQ.
8. At 1000 hours the 185th Brigade.

Despite 50 per cent casualties to the armoured vehicles, nine beach exits were opened by 1130 hours, though stubborn German resistance on the Periers Ridge (the strongpoint HILLMAN and the radar station at Douvres are on the ridge) was holding up movement inland, preventing the 185th Brigade from getting on towards Caen. The German resistance on the Periers Ridge leeched away the armour strength needed for the drive to Caen, where the 21st Panzer Division was gathering itself to strike.

Walk 100 yards east to the tank.

The **Churchill AVRE** was presented to Hermanville on 6 June 1987 by 3rd British Armoured Division. Beside it is a **NTL Totem** telling the story of Major General Rennie's 3rd Infantry Division.

Over the road is La Chapelle de la Brêche d'Hermanville, in which there is a colourful 4 metres high **stained glass window** which recalls the sacrifice of those who fought for the town's liberation. It depicts Christ on the Cross, surrounded by parachutes, aeroplanes and ships, with soldiers of June 1944 at his feet. The Chapel is often used for D-Day Landings and other exhibitions.

Return to your car and take the road past the chapel, the D60B rue du 6 Juin signed to Hermanville. Continue into the village and stop in the square by the church.

• Hermanville: Medical HQ Well, CWGC Cemetery (Lat & Long: 49.28619 -0.30872), 3rd Div HQ, Harold Pickersgill Tree/5.5 miles/30 minutes

On the left is a well with a Plaque which explains that this was the well of the Mare Saint Pierre which is said to have supplied 1,500,000 gallons of water to the British Forces between 6th June and 1st July 1944.

Turn left along the narrow road signed Cimetière Britannique.

Continue to **Hermanville CWGC Cemetery** in Place des Combattants 6 juin 1944.

There are 1,005 burials in this beautiful cemetery, many of them from the 6 June actions in this area. There are 986 British, 13 Canadian, 3 Australian and 3 French. There is a pair of **brothers, Lieutenant Alan Law Davis,** 5th Battalion the W Yorks Regiment, age 24, Plot II Row O Grave 10, and **CSM Norman Clave Davis**, 5th Battalion the King's Regiment of Liverpool, age 28, Plot II Row O Grave 7, who were both killed on 6 June, and in Plot I Row J Grave 15 *Croix de Guerre* winner the **Rev Peter Francis Firth**, Chaplain First Class to the Forces, age 33, killed on 7 June.

Return to the square and continue 100 yards to the Mairie on the right.

On the left of the gatepost is a **Plaque** commemorating **3rd British Infantry Division HQ** set up here on D-Day and on the right a plaque to an important hospital centre. Over the road in front of the *Salle Polyvalente* is a green **Plaque** in front of a small oak tree which was planted in memory of **Citizen of Honour**

Local school children, Hermanville CWGC Cemetery.

Harold Pickersgill who died in 1998. In 1943 Harold worked on the highly secret exercise PINWE - Problems of the Invasion of North West Europe - making detailed maps of the Normandy area. Much of the information for the maps was supplied by members of the French Resistance. In June 1944 he insisted on landing at la Brêche (part of the coast whose defences he knew so well from his secret work) with his old regiment, the Reconnaissance Corps, 3rd Division. Always active in liaising between his old division and the local authorities for commemorative events, Harold himself received an MBE in 1984. The Plaque was erected by the active HMS (*Histoire, Mémoire, Souvenir*) Association of Hermanville-sur-Mer.

Continue through the village to the D60/D35 junction and turn left on the D35. signed to Colleville-Montgomery. Drive determinedly into the centre of Colleville-Montgomery and at the main crossroads turn right hopefully following signs to 'Hillman Blockhouse' (signing can be challenging). Continue on Rue du Régiment Suffolk to the parking area beyond the blockhouse.

• HILLMAN Strong Point, 1st Battalion Suffolk Regiment Plaque/7.8 miles/30 minutes/Lat & Long: 49.26481 -0.30955

This strong defensive position covering 2,500 square yards protected by mines and wire and containing a concrete bunker and underground works, was the HQ of the German 736th Regiment with an area strength of more than 150 men. It was taken by the Suffolk Regiment, aided by two troops of Shermans of the 13th/18th Hussars after a six-hour battle in which the Suffolks had 20 men killed.

The **Plaque** on the bunker commemorates all those of the regiment who fell in the liberation of Colleville, the capture of HILLMAN and later fighting in Normandy. It pays tribute to the Colleville family who in February 1989 made this site available so that future generations could recognise the bravery and sacrifice of the soldiers. The complex has now been developed into an extensive and fascinating site, well worth a thorough visit. To the right as one approaches the Bunker is an Information Panel with a sketch map. On top of the Bunker is an Orientation Table showing the bunker system built by the Germans between 1942 and 1944. To the right is a meadow around which are scattered Information Panels on concrete pillars describing points of interest, such as the well that supplied the complex, the reservoir, 'Bunker Hunter DCM' (Col Krug's 736th Gren Regt Command Post) etc. Looking out from the car park, beside which is an **NTL totem**, the tall buildings of the Colombelles steel works can be seen on the horizon. To a first approximation they mark the area of Pegasus Bridge and the glider landings of John Howard's *Coup de Main*.

The area has been developed by 'The Friends of the Suffolk Regiment', a local Association based on the *Mairie* of Colleville-Montgomery. Tel: +(0)2 31 97 12 61. Fax: +(0)2 31 97 44 63. Website: www.amis-du-suffolk-rgt.com
E-mail: suffolk@amis-du-suffolk-rgt.com   Guided visits every Tuesday from 1500.

Return to the village crossroads and go straight over on the D60A Rue de la Mer and continue keeping as straight as possible to the T junction with the D514 coast road and the statue on the right.

• General Montgomery Statue, Anglo-French Forces/First British Graves, Naming of Colleville-Montgomery Memorials/No 4 Commando Memorial/10.0 miles/15 minutes

In the square is the bronze statue of General Montgomery sculpted by Vivien Mallock (qv), to which the statue in Portsmouth (qv) is identical. It was unveiled on 6 June 1996 by Prince Michael of Kent and was presented to Colleville-Mongomery by the Normandy Veterans' Association. The *Commune* of Colleville donated the land on which the statue stands. At night the statue is illuminated.

Walk over the road.

To the left on either side of the road leading to the beach - Avénue du No 4 Commando - are two Memorials. One erected on 6 June 1945 commemorates the first British graves of 6 June 1944, the Anglo-French forces of General Montgomery and Capitaine Kieffer of No 10 (Inter-Allied) Commando and the decision of Colleville-sur-Mer to change its name to Colleville-Montgomery. On the other side of the road is another memorial to Commandant Kieffer and the French forces of No. 10 Commando.

[**N.B.** By driving down this road to the promenade and turning left along rue Vauban is a stone bas relief **Monument to No 4 Cdo** including 177 French Commandos of 1st Bn French Marine Commando under Cdt Kieffer who landed here, which was inaugurated in 1994. Carved by Patrick Gheleyns it vividly depicts the Commandos' landing and the heavy and fearful casualties they endured. '*Notre liberté fut a ce prix!*' is the inscription. In the top left hand corner is a Plaque **to the Royal Norfolks** and on the ground a bronze Plaque which relates how the French Commandos landed followed by Nos 3 and 6 and 45 RM Cdo. A new stone was added on 6 June 2004.]

Continue on the D514 to the western edge of Ouistreham and at the cross roads turn left along Boulevard Winston Churchill and then right following signs to La Plage, Casino and Musée. At the small roundabout by the splendid *****Hotel des Thermes Thalassotherapie** Centre, 89 rooms. Thalassotherapy pool and treatments. **Restaurant Thalazur** Riva Bella. Tel: +(0)2 31 96 40 40. E-mail: ouistreham@thalazur.fr

Turn left and stop at the memorial on the right.

• No 4 Commando, Kieffer Memorials, Musée du No 4 Commando, Ouistreham-Riva-Bella/11.5 miles/20 minutes

The central task of 1st SS (Special Service) Brigade was to land in the Ouistreham area, to clear the town and then to move on to link up with the airborne forces at Pegasus Bridge. The Brigade, under command of 3rd British Division, was made up as follows:

Brigade Commander. Brigadier The Lord Lovat, DSO MC

No 3 Commando. Lieutenant-Colonel P. Young, DSO MC

No 4 Commando. Lieutenant-Colonel R.W.F. Dawson.

No 6 Commando. Lieutenant-Colonel D. Mills-Roberts, DSO MC.

No 45 RM Commando. Lieutenant-Colonel N.C. Ries

Nos 1 & 8 French Troops of No 10 Inter-Allied Commando. Captain Philippe Kieffer. In addition, No 41 RM Commando (Lieutenant-Colonel T.M. Gray) also came under command but had an independent role at Lion-sur-Mer.

No 4 Commando landed at 0820 hours on QUEEN Beach Red sector and came under heavy fire, suffering about forty casualties. Lieutenant-Colonel Robert Dawson was wounded in the leg and in the head but No 4 Commando reached the D514 and set off towards Ouistreham, led by Philippe Kieffer. A local gendarme whom they met on route gave them details of German strengths and positions and after a fierce fight ending with grenades and bayonets, in which both sides sustained many casualties, Kieffer's men took the Casino, an action that was made much of in the film *The Longest Day*. The casino building itself had been demolished by the Germans in October 1942 and replaced with concreted gun positions which were taken on by a Centaur prior to the final assault. No

HILLMAN Blockhouse,
Periers Ridge.

Atlantic Wall
Museum,
Ouistreham.

4 Cdo & Cdt Kieffer 'Flame'
Memorial, Ouistreham.

Gen Montgomery Statue,
Colleville-Montgomery.

4 Cdo Museum,
Ouistreham.

4 Commando then moved on towards Pegasus Bridge.

Lord Lovat, SS Brigade HQ and No 6 Commando landed on QUEEN Beach Red sector at 0820 hours, piped ashore by Piper Bill Millin. Artillery and mortar fire was considerable and three of their landing craft were hit. They moved rapidly inland, heading for Bréville to the east of Pegasus Bridge, clearing two pillboxes on the way. As they approached the bridge they waved a Union Flag in order to establish themselves as 'friendly forces' and were met by Brigadier J.H.N. Poett, the Commander of 5th Parachute Brigade. 'We are very pleased to see you', said Nigel Poett. 'I am afraid we are a few minutes late sir,' was the reply. Lovat and his men then moved over Pegasus Bridge to the cheers of the paratroopers and attracted considerable fire from German snipers.

No 3 and No 45 RM Commando landed at 0910 hours and moved inland and across the bridges over the Orne river and canal. No 45 went on to Merville while No 3 formed a protection force at Ranville for 6th AB Division HQ.

By the end of the day the 1st SS Brigade had not occupied the high ground east of the Orne, but they had cleared Ouistreham and fulfilled their main task of linking up with the airborne forces. They had also found out that French civilians were not too enthusiastic about their shoulder patch, which said 'SS'. It was later changed.

On the dunes is a **Memorial** to the memory of **ten members of Kieffer's Commandos** and to **No 4 Commando**. It is a symbolic flame erected in 1984 on top of a German blockhouse cupola. At its base is a bas relief **Memorial to Commandant Philippe Kieffer**.

Continue to the junction, take the first left and turn left again. Continue to the Casino square and park by the Museum on the right.

By the Casino is the **Tourist Office**. Tel: +(0)2 31 97 18 63. E-mail: office.ouistreham@wanadoo.fr website: www.ville-ouistreham.fr The Casino has two **Restaurants: Le Doris**, with seaview and **Le Bistro** (Fri, Sat, Sun) with dancing/live shows, Tel: +(0)2 31 36 30 30.

Beside it is the **Bar-Brasserie-Crêperie/Saladerie L'Accostage**. Tel: +(0)2 31 97 05 23. Open every day and provides a good value snack/lunch when others may be closed. Closed Tuesday out of season.

The Museum, now signed as *Musée du Débarquement* as well as of **No 4 Commando**, was organised by a group of citizens of Ouistreham who wished to preserve the memory of the events of the landings here. It has exhibits of arms, uniforms, badges and souvenirs. There is a film of the landings. Outside is a propeller from a Wellington which was recovered from the sea. There is also a **NTL Totem** which describes how 123 houses and villas were demolished by the Germans in the construction of the impressive defensive system here.

Open: Every day March – end October 1030-1800. Entrance fee payable. Tel: +(0)2 31 96 63 10.

Continue past the museum and take the road 'Boulevard 6 juin' straight ahead signed Musée du Mur de l'Atlantique. 400 yards later stop by the large concrete building/ museum on the left.

• *Musée le Mur de l'Atlantique/12.2 miles/20 minutes/Lat & Long: 49.28723 -0.25268*

This 52-feet-high concrete tower is the only major German work left in Ouistreham. It was a flak tower designed to control anti-aircraft defence of the harbour and was the German HQ in charge of the batteries covering the entrance of the River Orne and the Orne Canal. On 6 June the Franco-British commandos attempted to take the tower but were repulsed by machine-gun fire and stick grenades. It remained a threat until on 9 June Lieutenant Bob Orrell of 91st Field Company RE with three men placed explosive charges by the heavily armoured door which eventually burst open. The garrison of 2 officers and 50 men then surrendered. Since 1987 when it was fully restored the tower has been a museum in which one can see the generator room, the gas filter rooms, the machine gun emplacements, telephone exchange, radio transmission room and observation post. There are also many unpublished photographs and documents about the Atlantic Wall which employed over 2 million people in its construction. In September 1942 Hitler held a meeting with Speer (Minister for Armaments), von Rundstedt, Goering and others at which he specified a defensive coastal wall that would stretch from Norway to the Spanish border and consist of 15,000 strongpoints manned by 300,000 troops. In the grounds is a rare V1 with other interesting exhibits and a **NTL Totem**.

Open: daily from 12 February - 15 November 1000-1200 and 1400-1800 (from 1 June-30 September 0900-1900). Tel: +(0)2 31 97 28 28 69.

Continue straight on, and turn right on the coast road passing on the left the **Ferry Terminal.** *Tel: 08 03 82 88 28. In the car park is*

• *Royal Naval & Royal Marine Memorial/13.4 miles/10 minutes*

On 6 June 2000 a major omission was redressed when, during an impressive ceremony, HRH Prince Philip, Duke of Edinburgh, unveiled a handsome 6-foot-high granite Memorial bearing the names of the **RM and RN D-Day casualties**, the Combined Operations badge and a kedge anchor. The Memorial, which cost £18,000 was instigated by Maurice A. Hillebrandt, who served with Combined Operations RN.

On the right is the conveniently sited *****Hotel Mercure Riva Bella**. Renovated. 49 rooms. Tel: +(0)2 31 96 20 20. E-mail: H1967@accor.com

On the harbour wall to the left can be seen a 'Maginot Line' type cupola and vestiges of two pontoons.

Continue to the large square with ample parking around (Place Général de Gaulle).

Here there is a good choice of hotels, restaurants, newsagents and shops.

Follow Autres Directions, then Caen and continue to the roundabout.

• *Comité du Débarquement Monument, No 4 Commando Plaque/14.4 miles/5 minutes/Lat & Long: 49.26785 -0.26221*

In the roundabout is a *Comité du Débarquement Signal* Monument, which until 1987 stood on the harbour at Ouistreham. At the back of the memorial is a **Plaque** to the **French** and **British commandos** of **No 4 Commando**.

• *END OF ITINERARY FIVE*

ITINERARY SIX
BRITISH AIRBORNE OPERATIONS

There were two types of airborne soldiers, classified according to the way in which they landed - by parachute or by glider. Thus there were two types of zones in which they would come down - dropping zones [DZs] for parachutists and landing zones [LZs] for gliders.

6th AIRBORNE DIVISION LANDINGS

Drop Time:	0020 hours *coup-de-main* on Pegasus Bridge.
	0050 hours 3rd & 5th Parachute Brigades.
Leading Formations:	3rd and 5th Parachute Brigades of 6th
	Airborne Division.
6th AB Division Commander:	Major General R.N. ('Windy') Gale
German Defenders:	716th Infantry Division
716th Division Commander:	Lieutenant General Wilhelm Richter

The Plan - 6th Airborne Division Landings

The airborne plan was scheduled to begin before the main landings, and in darkness, in order to achieve the maximum surprise. The earliest troops into Normandy were, where possible, to be paratroopers who would be less sensitive to obstacles than their comrades in gliders. The paratroopers were to clear landing areas for later glider landings. The tasks were distributed between two brigade groups on a geographical basis as follows:

5th Parachute Brigade Group (Brigadier J.H.N. Poett) comprising the 7th, 12th and 13th Parachute Battalions, D Company of the Oxfordshire and Buckinghamshire Light Infantry and supporting arms and services was to:

1. Seize the bridges over the Orne using six gliders manned by the Oxfordshire and Buckinghamshire Light Infantry and
2. Seize and hold the area of Pegasus Bridge and Ranville and clear the LZs north of Ranville for glider reinforcements. They were to land on DZ'N' with elements of the 7th Parachute Battalion on DZ 'W'.

3rd Parachute Brigade Group (Brigadier James Hill) comprising the 1st Canadian Parachute Battalion, 8th and 9th Parachute Battalions and supporting arms and services was to:

1. Destroy the Merville Battery 1½ hours before the first landing craft were due and
2. Destroy a number of bridges (e.g. at Varaville, Robehomme, Bures and Troarn) over the River Dives and thus prevent the enemy from attacking Ranville from the eastern flank.

They were to land on DZ 'K' and DZ 'V'.

What happened on D-Day - 6th Airborne Division Landings

The leading planes of 38th and 46th Groups of the Royal Air Force carried men of the 22nd Independent Parachute Company whose job it was to mark the dropping and landing zones. With them went the RAF Commander, Air Vice Marshal L.N. Hollinghurst, and on time the pathfinders jumped out into the night sky.

At the same time as the pathfinders flew over their objectives the *coup-de-main* party of Ox and Bucks led by Major John Howard landed three of their gliders beside the Orne

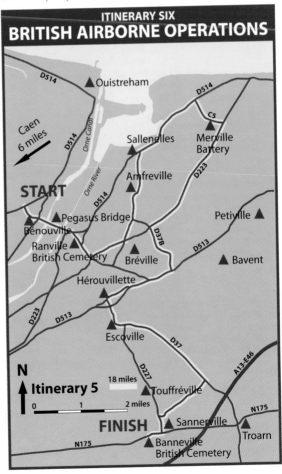

Canal. In ten minutes Pegasus Bridge was theirs.

By the end of the day both Orne bridges were in Allied hands, despite German counter-attacks, Ranville and the DZs were secure, a link-up had been made with Lord Lovat's Special Service Brigade from SWORD Beach, bridges over the River Dives at Troarn, Bures, Robehomme and over a tributary of the Dives at Varaville had been blown and the Merville Battery had been put out of action, despite a bad start. 6th AB Division had achieved its objectives, but it was thinly spread. The 6 June may have been the longest day for the men of the airborne forces but there was another one tomorrow and the Panzers were coming. The 7th could be longer.

THE BATTLEFIELD TOUR

[You may wish to visit the **Caen Mémorial Museum** before starting this itinerary. **Lat & Long: 49.198095 -0.383641**

It is reached from the Périphérique by taking Exit 7 and following clear signs.

This vast and important, high-tech **Museum**, opened in 1988 and funded mostly by American money, is set in Memorial Gardens. It covers themes such as pre-War Normandy, the Occupation, the Landings, the Battle of Normandy, the Resistance, the reconstruction, Nobel Peace Prize Winners, with much use of filmed material. Cafeteria and well-stocked shop. **Open:** daily 0900-1900 (0930-1800 in winter) except 25 Dec and 4-26 Jan. Tel: + +(0)2 31 06 06 44. E-mail: resa@memorial-caen.fr Website: www.memorial-caen.fr Entrance fee payable. Allow 2 hours for a full visit.]

THE TOUR STARTS AT BÉNOUVILLE/PEGASUS BRIDGE

It covers the 6th AB Div glider and parachute operations.

* Planned duration without stops for refreshments or extra visits: 4 hours 30 minutes
* Total distance: 18 miles

*Pegasus Bridge may be reached from the Caen ring road (Périphérique, N13) by following signs to Ouistreham and Car Ferry on the D515/D84, or from Ouistreham on the D514. Take the exit signed to Bénouville on the D514. Continue over the roundabout and park on the right before the Pegasus (Gondrée) Café on 'Avénue du Commandant Kieffer'. **Set your mileometer to Zero.***

The Pegasus Bridge Café.

- *Bénouville/Mairie Plaque, 7th Light Infantry Battalion Plaque, Gondrée Café, Cromwell Tank, 1st Bailey Bridge Marker, Bénouville Bridge, Ox and Bucks Plaque, Comité du Débarquement Monument, John Howard Bust, Glider Landings Markers, Pegasus Mémorial Museum, Original Bridge, Replica Horsa, Brig Hill statue, Brotheridge Memorial/0 miles/1 hour*

On the *Mairie* by the roundabout behind you is a **Plaque** commemorating it as the **first Mairie to be liberated**. Gallic enthusiasm insists that liberation came at 2345 hours on 5 June '*par les parachutistes anglais*'.

On the corner diagonally opposite the *Mairie*, at the foot of a religious stone memorial, is a **Plaque** in memory of **7th Light Infantry Battalion of the Parachute Regiment**. The 7th were scattered by the strong winds and shot at by the Germans as they dropped but their CO, Lieutenant-Colonel Pine-Coffin, using his bugler who dropped with him, rallied a force of about 200 and by 0300 established a defence perimeter around the bridge.

The plan to take the two bridges over the Orne was that six gliders carrying airborne soldiers of the Ox and Bucks under command of Major John Howard would land between them. John Howard told his glider pilots that he wanted the leading machine to land within 50 yards of the canal bridge. Three gliders were to go for one bridge and three for the other. Howard himself was to be in the force attacking the canal bridge (immediately ahead of you) with a platoon of some thirty men in each glider.

At 2256 hours on 5 June the little armada, towed by Halifax bombers, took off. In glider No 1, flown by Jim Wallwork, John Howard sat beside Den Brotheridge and they all practised the code words meaning that the bridges had been captured - 'HAM' for the canal bridge and 'JAM' for the river bridge.

The journey over was uneventful and some seven miles from the bridges the tugs released the gliders. Now it was up to the pilots, and this is how John Howard remembers the landing:

'……..the skids seared through the ground and sent up sparks as the metal skids hit flints and it looked like tracer fire flashing past the door causing inevitable thought of surprise lost. Airborne again and suddenly there was to be the last searing God Almighty crash amidst smashing plywood, dust and noise like hell let loose, followed by sudden silence as we came to a halt. The dazed silence did not seem to last long because we all came to our senses together on realising that there was NO firing. There WAS NO FIRING, it seemed quite unbelievable……. All I can remember was as I stood clear of the mangled glider I saw the tower of the canal bridge no more than 50 yards away, and the nose of the glider right through the enemy wire defences - precisely where I had asked the GPs to put it during briefing. To cap it all there was NO enemy firing. The sense of complete exhilaration was quite overwhelming! I automatically looked at my watch, it had stopped at 0016 hours.

The paratroopers threw grenades into the pill box at the end of the bridge and Den Brotheridge led his men at a run over to the other side. Sadly he was killed. The most spectacular operation of D-Day had lasted barely 10 minutes. Total casualties were two killed and fourteen wounded. The airborne had taken Pegasus Bridge and the Germans never re-took it, and M Gondrée who owned the café at the end of the bridge dug up some hidden champagne to celebrate.

Pegasus Café. Lat & Long: 49.2426 -0.2751. Within the first hours of D-Day, the Café quickly became a first aid post. The café, which is a listed historic building, is owned and run by Madame Gondrée's daughter Arlette (who as a child was in the Café on 6 June 1944) It serves snacks and light meals and sells appropriate books and souvenirs. **Open: daily** 13 March – 12 November. Tel/Fax: +(0)2 31 44 62 25. In the grounds of the Pegasus Café is a **NTL Totem**.

Over the road is a Centaur A27M Cromwell tank of **5 (Independent) RM Armd Spt Bty**. It came ashore at la Brèche d'Hermanville, where it was put out of action. It was recovered in November 1975 and brought to the Pegasus Bridge area in June 1977.

Continue over the new bridge, drive to the Pegasus Memorial Museum, park in the car park and walk back to the bridge.

The original bridge was replaced in April 1994. The new bridge is essentially the same shape and design as the original but is longer and wider. On the bank of the Canal, known as the 'Esplanade John Howard', is a complex of memorials to the events of 5-6 June. On the bridge is a **Plaque** to commemorate the action of the **2nd (Airborne) Battalion Ox and Bucks** who captured Pegasus Bridge in the night of 5-6 June 1944, erected by their heirs the Royal Green Jackets. On the bank is a German 50mm anti-tank gun and beside it is a *Comité du Débarquement* **Monument** and an Orientation Table.

The bronze **bust of John Howard** was sculpted by Vivien Mallock (qv) and presented to the mayor and citizens of Bénouville by the Ox and Bucks Light Infantry Association and the Airborne Assault Normandy Trust in June 1995.

In the low ground behind are three lectern-like glider markers. They were unveiled in June 1977 by General Gale. They show exactly where each of John Howard's gliders landed, and give details of their crews and passengers, and precise time of landing.

The **old Pegasus Bridge** is in the grounds of the **Airborne Museum, Memorial Pegasus, Lat & Long: 49.2426 -0.2751**, opened on 4 June 2000 by Prince Charles, Colonel in Chief of the Parachute Regiment. The custom-built modern structure, whose roof is shaped like a glider, was sponsored by the *Comité du Débarquement*, the *Communes* of Bénouville and Ranville, the *Département* and the Region and it commemorates the actions around the Orne bridges, especially by 6th Airborne on 5/6 June 1944. In it are the main exhibits from the original Pegasus Museum plus many new items and models. There is a smart boutique with a good stock of books, maps and souvenirs. In the grounds is an **original Bailey Bridge** (one of 30 or so built by the REs in the area in 1944). It stands beside the old Pegasus Bridge upon which is **a Plaque to Lance Corporal Brian J. Mullen**, Sapper RE, No 4 Commando Intelligence Section. Corporal Mullen is buried in Hermanville CWGC Cemetery. On 5 June 2004 Prince Charles unveiled a unique full size replica Horsa Glider in the grounds.

Original Pegasus Bridge, Museum grounds.

Pegasus Memorial Museum.

Beside it are two small hangars – one with part of an original Horsa, the other a glider exhibition complete with John Howard's personal commentary. A **Memorial to Lt Den Brotheridge** was also unveiled. In 2005 a **statue** by Vivien Mallock (qv) of **Brig James Hill, DSO, MC**, *Légion d'Honneur*, US Silver Star, King Haakon's Norwegian Liberty Cross, was moved here from its original site at l'Arbre Martin to preserve it from vandalism.

Open: daily from 1 May-30 September 0930-1830, 1 October – 30 November and 1 February – 30 April 1000-1300 and 1400-1700. **Closed** 1 December – 31 January. Entrance fee payable. Tel: +(0)2 31 78 19 44. Fax: +(0)2 31 78 19 42. E-mail: memorial.pegasus@wanadoo.fr

Continue on the D514 to the pedestrian crossing before the bridge over the river on the left.

• Memorial to the Horsa Bridge Glider Landings/0.4 miles/5 minutes

The Memorial, in French and English, tells the story of the capture of the bridge which was named 'Horsa' after the gliders used by the airborne forces. The enemy defending it had run away leaving their weapons behind.

One of those who jumped into Normandy that morning was Lieutenant Richard Todd who landed just before 0100 hours. Both he and Lieutenant Sweeney who landed with the gliders told the same story about how they met each other on Pegasus Bridge. Lieutenant Sweeney's version was, 'I met this chap on the bridge and he said, "Hello, my name is Todd and they call me Sweeney", so I replied, "Hello, my name is Sweeney and they call me Todd"'.

Continue to the roundabout and take the D37 signed to Ranville. Take the next turning right on the rue de la Vallée and then immediately left heading for Ranville church. Drive just beyond the church to the Commonwealth War Graves Commission Cemetery. Stop on the left. There are a number of visits that can be made on foot:-

• *Ranville CWGC Cemetery, Airborne, Piron Brigade, Maj Strafford Plaque and other Memorials, General Gale Bust/1.2 miles/20 minutes*

The capture of the Ranville area was the responsibility of the 13th (Lancashire) Parachute Battalion of Nigel Poett's 5th Brigade.

The cemetery was begun by Royal Engineers of 591st Parachute Squadron RE, who put up wooden crosses, which remained until after the war. Today there are 2,563 burials, including 323 Germans. To the left of the War Stone almost in the centre of the cemetery is a stone cross bearing a bronze plaque with the emblem of the Airborne Forces on it and remembering simply, 'June 1944'. This was erected in September 1944 by Royal Engineers of 1st AB Division. Inside and to the left of the gateway is a **Memorial Seat to 9th Parachute Battalion**. On the other side of the gateway is a **Memorial Seat to 8th Midland Counties Parachute Battalion**, dedicated on 5 June 1988. The Seat by the entrance to the local churchyard was presented by the **Thanet Branch of the Airborne Forces Association** in June 1986. Buried in Plot IIIA, Row L is the poet **Major William John Fletcher Jarmain**, of 193 Battery 61st Anti-tank Regiment, RA.

Stand squarely in front of the main entrance to the cemetery and take that direction as 12 o'clock.

Next to the cemetery is Ranville church. Opposite is a **NTL Totem**. Around the inside of the wall on the far side of the church there are 48 contemporary war graves, including one German and two French soldiers and **Lieutenant Den Brotheridge**, who was killed at Pegasus Bridge. Behind Brotheridge's headstone is a commemorative plaque placed by the Gondrée family acknowledging him as the first Allied soldier killed during the landings. In the cemetery is buried **Bombardier H. Hall** whose date of death is given as 5 June 1944, presumably because he - and so many others - were killed at sea or in the air on the way over the Channel.

CWGC Cemetery, Ranville.

Immediately opposite the entrance to the CWGC Cemetery is a low wall on which is a map and a concise summary of the airborne operations in the area, erected by **1 Field Squadron RE** which lists the units involved in the actions. On the stone tower is a **Plaque in memory of the Belgian Piron Brigade** which formed an 'Allied' element of the 2nd British Army together with a Czech armoured brigade, a Netherlands brigade and a Polish Armoured Division. Behind the tower is a **Memorial to Major Charles Strafford MBE** of HQ 6th AB Division, 1914 -1993.

In the garden of the *Mairie*, in front of the Bibliothèque (Library), is a striking **bust of General Sir Richard Gale**, 1896-1982, sculpted by Vivien Mallock. It was presented in June 1994 by the Airborne Assault Association and the Normandy Trust. Below it is an old plaque proclaiming that Ranville was the first village liberated at 0230 on 6 June 1944 by the **13th (Lancashire) Battalion** the Parachute Regiment. This is the original, damaged version, of the plaque next visited.

Drive down the road past the Mairie to the first crossroads in the village.

Here on the wall is the second plaque.

Continue straight over on the D223 and then to the first crossroads. Turn left and then left again on the C10 to Amfreville. On entering the village turn left, signed Sallenelles on the D37b and continue to where the road divides either side of a green in the centre of which is a church. Stop just before the division by a memorial on the right.

• No 6 Commando Memorial, Amfreville/3.2 miles/5 minutes

Beyond the Memorial to No 6 Commando is a **NTL Totem**.

The bridgehead established by the Airborne Forces in this area and reinforced by the 1st Special Service Brigade (re-named No 1 Commando Brigade in June 1944) was under constant counter-attack for almost two months and the commandos took heavy casualties from artillery fire.

The farm buildings to the right of the Memorial belong to farmer Bernard Saulnier who became a great friend of the Commandos. On 12 June a major offensive was launched through Amfreville's commando positions by 12th Parachute Battalion and elements of the Devonshire Regiment in an attempt to capture Bréville. Lord Lovat was seriously wounded by a high explosive shell and Bernard Saulnier carried him into one of his cowsheds leaving Lieutenant-Colonel Mills-Roberts in command for the rest of the war. Mills-Roberts died in 1980 and in 1988 his ashes were transferred to Normandy and buried by Bernard Saulnier in Bavent.

Continue left of the church to the memorial on the right.

• 1st Special Service Brigade Memorial/3.3 miles/5 minutes

The white cross, with explanatory Plaques each side, behind which are flagpoles, commemorates **1st Special Service Brigade's** part in the action here.

Follow the road around the green.

It is known as the 'Le Plain Place du Commandant Kieffer' and there is a sign over the entrance to the *Mairie* to that effect.

Take the north-eastern exit from the green, the D37b Route de Sallenelles, and drive slowly (about .3 mile) so as not to miss the left turn along rue Patra. Continue to the memorial at the end.

• No 4 Commando Memorial, Place Colonel Robert Dawson, Hoger/3.9 miles/5 minutes

Since 1944 many place names in Normandy have changed or been amalgamated with others. In British accounts of actions the Anglicised versions of French names are often used offering yet another spelling to confuse the reader. The village here, now awash with new houses, was known in 1944 as 'Hauger' to the British.

This area is also known as le Hoger and on 10 June particularly intense fighting here involving No 4 Commando led to one troop losing all its officers. German counter-attacks on the high ground of Hoger - Le Plain - Amfreville had begun on the afternoon of 6 June and continued incessantly for four days.

The **Memorial Cairn to No 4 Commando** is in Place Colonel Robert Dawson (named on a **Memorial Plaque**). It bears a slightly modified quotation from the Marquis of Montrose,

'He either fears his fate too much,
Or his deserts are small,
Who dare not [sic] put it to the touch,
To win or lose it all.'

Colonel Dawson commanded No 4 but was twice wounded while landing on the beaches. On 7 June he rejoined the Commandos but on 9 June the medical officer ordered him to the rear. The château over the wall was, for a time, the No 4 Commando HQ though the first Allied occupants of the château had been Lieutenant-Colonel Terence Otway and the remnants of the 9th Parachute Battalion who made their way here having taken the Merville Battery.

Return to the D37b, turn left passing rue du 4ième Commando on the right and continue towards Sallenelles. Stop on the right, just beyond the Sallenelles sign, near house No 23.

• 4th Special Service Brigade HQ Memorial, Sallenelles/4.6 miles/5 minutes

The **Memorial** commemorates **Nos 41, 46, 47 and 48 RM Commandos** whose headquarters were here from June- August 1944.

Continue into Sallenelles and turn right on the D514 signed to Merville and continue some 50 yards to house no 13-15.

• Edouard Gérard, Belgian Memorial/4.9 miles/5 minutes

On the gate post of the house is a **Plaque** to the memory of **Edouard Gérard** of the 1st Piron Brigade. He was the first Belgian soldier to be killed in Normandy - on 16 August 1944.

Continue to the end of the village and turn left immediately after the Mairie on the left. Ahead is

• Piron Brigade Memorial/5.0 miles/5 minutes

The **Memorial** commemorates the **Belgian and Luxembourgois Brigade** of Colonel Jean Piron, 14 August 1944, with the names of soldiers at the bottom.

Continue on the D514 following signs to Merville-Franceville-Plage. to the traffic lights in Merville and turn right at the sign for la Battérie de Merville and stop immediately on the right by the group of memorials.

• No 45 RM Commando, Liberators/Civilians, Piron Memorials, Merville/6.5 miles/10 minutes

On the left of the group is a black marble **Memorial** to the **35 soldiers of No 45 RM Commando** killed in Merville on 8 June 1944. Beside it is the cream stone Merville-Franceville memorial to their dead and their liberators and a grey marble memorial to the 'Allied Soldiers and the Civilians of Merville-Franceville' who fell during June and July 1944. On the right is a grey marble **Memorial** to two sergeants and two soldiers of the **Piron Brigade** killed on 18 August.

Continue following signs to the Merville Battery and stop by the main gate.

• Merville Battery/Museum/9th Parachute Battalion Memorial, Colonel Otway Bust/7.2 miles/45 minutes/Lat & Long: 49.27020 -0.19654

At the entrance to the battery complex is a **Memorial to 9th Parachute Battalion** and opposite it a **NTL Totem**. There is also a Plaque to **No 3 Commando**. There are **Plaques** on the trees to members of the Battalion who died after the war, including **Lt-Col Terence Otway** who died on 23 July 2006, age 93. He received the *Légion d'Honneur* in 2001.

At this spot the diversionary action (qv) was made and there are a number of

The 'SNAFU Special' Dakota, Merville Battery.

Casemate No 1,
Merville Battery.

Information Boards and diagrams explaining what happened. The area is owned by the *Conservatoire du Littéral* who have preserved the 5-hectare site since the end of the war. It is administered by a charitable trust whose director is Mme Pascaline Dagorn with strong support from the Mayor Olivier Paz. This is one of the most innovative sites in Normandy and it merits a thorough visit.

One enters through a reception/boutique area which sells books, souvenirs etc. **Open:** 1 April-30 Sept every day 1000-1800, 15-31 March and 1-31 October Mon, Wed and weekends 1000-1700. Entrance fee payable. Tel: +(0)2 31 91 47 53. E-mail: museebatterie@wanadoo.fr Website: www.batterie-merville.com There are toilets at the back of Casemate No 1.

A powerful sound, light and odour experience was inaugurated in April 2007 in Casemate No 1. Every half hour a siren sounds to announce the next performance which immerses the visitor into a deluge of combat – the hell that unfolded at dawn on 6 June 1944. There is a warning to those with heart conditions, claustrophobia or who are under age 8 that this may well be too overwhelming.

The most exciting acquisition in 2008 was a **Dakota 43-15073**, known as 'The SNAFU Special', which had flown several missions to Normandy, Holland and Germany in 1944/5 during Operations Neptune, Dragoon, Market, Repulse and Varsity. More details of this extraordinary enterprise can be seen on the website: www.snafu-special.com.

Inside the grounds is a **Memorial Seat to Frederick Scott Walker**, 9th Battalion and a **bust to Lieutenant-Colonel Terence Otway** sculpted by Vivien Mallock (in a similar style to that of John Howard at Pegasus bridge).

The capture of the battery here was given to the 9th Parachute Battalion under Lieutenant-Colonel T. B. H. Otway. In the weeks before D-Day the RAF bombed the area several times, but with no damage to any of the 4 casemates. The 130 men of 716th Regiment who manned the battery not only had concrete to protect them from aerial attack but any assault on the ground had to penetrate a minefield between two barbed wire fences.

Otway's plan to take the bunker was complex and involved a charge through the wire defences as three *coup de main* gliders landed inside the perimeter. The drop was scattered and barely 25% of his force arrived. They had only one Vickers machine gun and twenty Bangalore torpedoes between them. Then the gliders failed to arrive so Otway decided to get on with the job. Without engineer support or any mine-clearing equipment it was a case of charging both the wire and the minefield. The paratroopers went forward firing their sten guns from the hip, using the gaps in the wire and minefield caused by bombing, and blowing two more gaps using the Bangalore torpedoes. Meanwhile at the main gate a small party opened fire, hoping to cause a diversion. The Germans fought well, coming out of their bunkers to counter-attack. It was a short and bloody scrap. The cost to the battalion was heavy - seventy officers and men killed or wounded. The German garrison was reduced to twenty-two prisoners, all the rest were killed or wounded.

When the casemates were examined the guns were found to be old French 75mm weapons on wheels. The anticipated heavy weapons had not been installed. Nevertheless the guns were put out of action. The 9th Parachute Battalion had not finished its task, however. Now they had to head for the high ground around Amfreville. Otway led his men off and later in the day a combat group of the German 736th Grenadier Regiment regained Merville only to lose it the following day to an assault by No 3 Commando. Once again it was a fierce battle but the Germans were overcome. Almost immediately the enemy counter-attacked using self-propelled guns and drove the commandos out and back to Le Plain.

Open: 1 April-30 Sept every day 1000-1800, 15-31 March and 1-31 October Mon, Wed and weekends 1000-1700. Tel: +(0)2 31 91 47 53. E-mail: museebatterie@wanadoo.fr

> *Return to the T junction and turn right continuing in the original direction of travel to Descanneville. There turn right on to the D223 signed Bréville. Drive to the crossroads with the D37b in Bréville and stop before the crossroads and the memorial on the right-hand corner opposite the Mairie.*

• 12th Parachute/12th Devonshire Regiment Memorial, Grave of Captain Ward, Bréville/10.4 miles/10 minutes

During one of his inspection tours, Rommel had visited Bréville, planning his defence of the high ground from a viewpoint at the crossroads where you now are. That defence was formidable and, despite the best efforts of the commandos, paratroopers and 51st Highland Division, the Germans held on, giving ground reluctantly and at great cost to themselves and their attackers. Even by the start of Operation GOODWOOD some six weeks after D-Day, the British front line extended no further south than Bréville.

On D-Day, after completing their primary tasks, the 9th Parachute and the 1st Canadian Parachute Battalion headed for the high ground. 9th Battalion got to Hoger, which you passed earlier, and the 1st Battalion reached le Mesnil, which you pass later. Meanwhile No 4 Commando dug in at Hoger and No 6 established themselves between Le Plain and Bréville. The Germans held Bréville. It was a confused and irregular battlefield with opposing forces jumbled together.

The German formations in this area were the 346th and 711th Infantry Divisions and for three days after D-Day they mounted heavy counter-attacks against the lightly equipped airborne forces on the high ground. Despite an attack by No 6 Commando and No 1 (French) under Keiffer the Germans still held Bréville four days after D Day.

On 10th June the 5th Battalion The Black Watch was moved to the Château of St Côme to prepare for an assault. The château is some 500 yards south-east of where you are, down the D376 to your left. It is next on the itinerary. At 0430 hours on 11 June the Black Watch set off towards you on their first action in Normandy. It was over very quickly. The Germans opened up a barrage of mortar, assault and anti-aircraft guns and the Black Watch retired with some 200 casualties to where they had started.

General Gale determined to try again. He strengthened the paratroopers with a company of the 12th Battalion the Devonshire Regiment and a troop of Sherman tanks of the 13th/18th Hussars and ordered an attack for 2200 hours on 12 June. The mixed formations gathered around and in the church in Amfreville (where you were earlier) and awaited the preliminary bombardment. At about 2100 hours the barrage began, but some of it fell short onto Amfreville near Bernard Saulnier's farm and it seems highly likely that the shell burst that injured Lord Lovat was 'friendly fire'.

Bréville was captured, though the price was a high one - the Devons had had heavy casualties as they formed up to attack, possibly from our own artillery, losing thirty-five soldiers and their company commander. The paratroopers lost their CO, Lieutenant-Colonel A. P. Johnston, seven officers and 133 soldiers. The Memorial is to those who died here, with captions in English and French.

Beside it is a **NTL Totem**. The area is called Carrefour (crossroads) Airborne Division. In the churchyard opposite are the graves of **Captain H.W. Ward** of the 53rd (Worcestershire Yeomanry) Airlanding Light Regiment RA and **Private C.J.B Masters** of 12 Para Battalion, both killed on 12 June.

Turn left on the D37b signed Troarn for about 500 yards and stop on the left at the small track that leads to the Château St Côme.

• 9th Parachute Infantry Battalion Memorial, Royal Netherlands Bde Plaque, 51st Highlander Statue/10.8 miles/5 minutes/Lat & Long: 49.23472 -0.22310

The Canadians, part of 3rd Parachute Brigade, dropped at DZ'V' in the area of Varaville, some 5 miles to the north-east of here. Their main task was to destroy the bridges over the River Dives in the region of Varaville and Robehomme. Despite being scattered over a wide area the Canadians blew the bridges and then moved through Château St Côme to a position at le Mesnil which is next on our route.

The **Memorial** here records in English and French what it calls the 'Battle of the Bois des Monts and the Château St Côme 7-13 June 1944', and describes the actions of the 9th Parachute Battalion, the attack by the Black Watch on Bréville and the involvement by the 1st Canadian Parachute Battalion until the force was relieved by the Ox and Bucks Light Infantry. Opposite it is a **Plaque** to the **Royal Netherlands Princess Irene Bde** who

51st Highland Div Piper,
Château St Côme.

liberated the area in August 1944. Across the road is a magnificent **Statue of a Highland soldier of the 51st (Highland) Division** sculpted by Alan B. Herriot. It commemorates the intense struggles of 10-12 June when the 5th Black Watch casualties included 110 killed. It was inaugurated on 5 June 2005.

Continue to the junction with the D513. Go straight over, signed Troarn, and stop immediately on the right in the car park by a grassy area.

• 1st Canadian Parachute Battalion Memorial, Place Brigadier James Hill, l'Arbre Martin/11.5 miles/10 minutes

Beside the Memorial to **1st Canadian Parachutists**, which reads, 'In tribute to all ranks of the 1st Canadian Parachute Battalion dropped into Normandy in the early hours of 'D'Day June 6 1944 who upon this ground successfully defended a vital approach to the east flank of the allied landings', is a stone with the sign to 'Square Brigadier James Hill'.

Return to the crossroads and turn left on the D513 signed Hérouvillette.

After some 250 yards is the area of le Mesnil, the rendezvous point for the 1st Canadian Parachute Battalion and other elements of 3rd Parachute Brigade whose task was to destroy bridges to the east around Varaville.

Continue and at 1 mile turn right into Hérouvillette on the D513a. After the church turn immediately left onto the rue de la Paix. Continue 100 yards to the cemetery entrance and stop.

• 2nd (Airborne) Battalion Oxfordshire & Buckinghamshire Light Infantry Plaque, Hérouvillette/12.9 miles/10 minutes

On the left of the entrance is the CWGC *'Tombes de Guerre'* (War Graves) sign and on the right a marble stone memorial originally dedicated on 6 June 1987 which says in English (and then in French):

'In Memory to those who fought at Pegasus Bridge, Escoville, Hérouvillette, Bréville les Monts and to the Seine and to the many brave French who helped us.'

In the cemetery are twenty-seven graves of airborne troops including Army Air Corps, RASC, the 12th Parachute Battalion and men of the Ox and Bucks Light Infantry.

This village was captured by the Ox and Bucks Light Infantry and the 1st Royal Ulster

(Left) *3rd Inf Div Memorial, Sannerville.*

(Below) *RM Cdo Memorial, Sannerville.*

Rifles on 7 June. They then went on the same day to attack Escoville, but were unsuccessful. Two days later the 21st Panzer Division counter-attacked Hérouvillette, but were driven off, after losing forty dead and four tanks and armoured cars.

Return to the D513, turn left over the mini roundabout and at the end of the village turn left again onto the D37 signed Troarn. Continue to Escoville and stop in front of the church in Place Six Juin 1944.

Entrance to CWGC Cemetery, Banneville-la-Campagne.

• Memorial to British Liberators, Escoville/13.8 miles/5 minutes

This commemorates the liberation in July 1944. In the churchyard is buried **Private William Wilkins** of the Ox and Bucks, who was killed on 7 June 1944.

Continue towards Troarn over the junction with the D37b and some 250 yards later on the left is a track leading left to the Manoir du Bois. Some 50 yards further on beside the road on the left are two memorials.

• 8th Parachute Battalion, Brigadier Alastair Pearson Memorials, Manoir du Bois/15.5 miles/10 minutes

The **Parachute Memorial** is a simple polished stone that says: 'In memory of all ranks of 8th Parachute Battalion 6 June-August 1944.'

Despite being scattered over several miles the 8th Battalion was able to blow bridges at Bures and at Troarn thanks mostly to the initiative of Major R.C.A. Roseveare RE who gathered a band of sappers and paras and set off. The second **Memorial** here was unveiled on 5 June 1996 and is to **Brigadier Alastair Pearson,** CB, DSO (3 bars), CBE, MC, TD, 1915-1996, who commanded 8th Parachute Battalion.

Continue on the D37 about .6 miles and turn right on the small road Le Maizeret. Stop at the memorial on the left.

• RM Cdo Memorial to Nos 41, 46, 47 and 48, Sannerville/16.5 miles/5 minutes/Lat & Long: 49.18991 -0.20668)

This was erected on 8 June 1991.

Continue on the small road to the church and memorial in Sannerville.

• 3rd Inf Div Memorial/Appleton Plaque, Sannerville/17.3 miles/5 minutes

The Division fought in the liberation of Caen. There is also a memorial Plaque to **Gp Capt Charles H. Appleton**, 124 Wing, RAF, killed 12 August 1944 and buried in Banneville-la-Campagne CWGC Cemetery visited next.

Continue and at the junction with the N175 turn right signed Démouville and continue to the parking area on the left.

• Banneville-la-Campagne CWGC Cemetery/18.00 miles/15 minutes/Lat & Long: 49.1765 -0.2294

The cemetery, designed by Philip Hepworth, contains 2,175 burials - 2,150 British, 11 Canadian, 5 Australian, 2 New Zealand, 5 Polish and 2 unidentified graves. They are mostly from the fighting of mid July-end August 1944 when Caen was captured and the Falaise Gap was closed. Here, in Plot III, Row F, Grave 22, is buried the artist **Lt Rex Whistler**, age 39, Welsh Guards, 18 July 1944. He was killed by a mortar shell on his first day in action.

End of Itinerary Six

ALLIED AND GERMAN WAR GRAVES & COMMEMORATIVE ASSOCIATIONS

THE AMERICAN BATTLE MONUMENTS COMMISSION (ABMC)

The Commission was established by the United States Congress in March 1923 for the permanent maintenance of military cemeteries and memorials on foreign soil. Their first task was to build cemeteries for the American dead of World War I.

After World War II, fourteen overseas military cemeteries were constructed, including the St Laurent Normandy Cemetery. They contain approximately 39 per cent of those originally buried in the region, the remaining 61 per cent were returned to the USA.

The ground on which each cemetery is built was granted by the host nation, free of rent or taxes. A white marble headstone marks every burial (Star of David for the Jewish, Latin cross for all others, whether they be Christian, Buddhist, agnostic or of any other belief). Memorials bearing the names of the missing, a non-denominational chapel and a visitors' room containing the register and visitors' book are standard in all cemeteries. All are open to the public daily.

The cemeteries are immaculately maintained by a superintendent (normally American) using local gardeners. He will supply photographs of the cemetery and the individual headstone for the next of kin and arrange for cut flowers to be bought locally and placed on the grave.

The Commission now maintains 24 permanent American burial grounds on foreign soil, in which there are 124,913 U.S. War Dead: 30,921 of WWI, 93,238 of WWII and 750 of the Mexican War. There are 25 separate memorials (3 of which are in the USA). The first Chairman, in 1923, was Gen John J. Pershing and in 2005 Gen Frederick M. Franks Jr was appointed.

For full details of the Normandy American Cemetery and Memorial, see Itinerary Two above. Other Americans who died in Normandy are buried in Saint James, south of Avranches on the N798 to Fougères. Called 'The Brittany Cemetery', it contains 4,410 burials and the names of 498 missing.

The Battle Monuments Commission offices are at:

UNITED STATES: Courthouse Plaza 11, Suite 500, 2300 Clarendon Boulevard, Arlington VA 22201. Tel: + 703 6966897.

FRANCE: 68 rue 19 janvier, 92 Garches, France. Tel: +(0)1 47 01 19 76.

Their website home page is www.abmc.gov. Their Roll of Honour website is www.abmc.gov/searchww.htm and one may now search for the names of casualties buried in American Cemeteries at the Visitor Centre at the Normandy American Cemetery.

ABMC Visitor Center, Normandy American Cemetery.

CANADIAN CEMETERIES

The Canadian cemeteries at Bény-sur-Mer and Bretteville-sur-Laize are maintained by the CWGC and are described below. Although primarily Canadian they both include some British and other nationalities. Canadians are also buried in Bayeux (181), Ryes (21), Tilly (1), Hottot (34), Fontenay (4), St. Manvieu (3), Brouay (2), La Délivrande (11), Hermanville (13), Ranville (76), Banneville (11), St Charles de Percy (3), and St Désir de Lisieux (16).

COMMONWEALTH WAR GRAVES COMMISSION

The story of the foundation of the Commonwealth War Graves Commission (CWGC) and its work after the Great War of 1914-18 is told in *Major & Mrs Holt's Battlefield Guides to the Ypres Salient and to the Somme*. After the Second World War, the Commission's task was two-fold: to restore the maintenance of the First World War Graves and to take on board the new task of commemorating the fallen from WWII. Conditions for the returning WWI gardeners, who had fled the invading Germans in 1940, were horrendous in war-torn Europe - often there was no housing, no food and the pay was pitiful. The story of the struggle is vividly told in Philip Longworth's *The Unending Vigil*. The inspiration and leading light of the Commission, Fabian Ware, was aging and ill. In November 1947 he resigned as Chairman, stayed on as theoretical Vice-Chairman, retired in June 1948 and died in April 1949 at the age of 80. There was no-one with his vision, practical experience and political acumen to succeed him. Ware is commemorated by a memorial plaque in the Warrior's Chapel at Westminster and in the naming of the principal ring-road around Bayeux.

Morale was at an all-time low as old problems were tackled anew and new ones emerged. Opinions as to the best way forward were mixed amongst the participating allies. New shaped headstones (examples of most of which can be seen in the polyglot

Bayeux Cemetery) had to be designed for the Czechs, the Poles, the French, the Norwegians, the Greeks, the Dutch, the Italians and the Belgians. The New Zealanders still refused to allow a personal message at the foot of the standard headstone. The Australians were loath to charge families for the inscription as had been the British policy after WWI. But by April 1946 all the old cemeteries in France and Belgium had been taken over once more and priority could then be given to the design and construction of the new cemeteries and memorials. The Army exerted pressure to create the new cemeteries as quickly as possible. By 1947 the existing staff proved inadequate for the task of tending 212,000 new graves. Work had begun in Normandy, where a CWGC

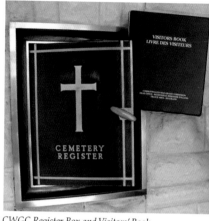

CWGC Register Box and Visitors' Book.

representative was posted in February 1946. The area was devastated, premises impossible to find. The Graves Registration Unit was operating from Bayeux and eventually they found some derelict garages on the coast. From there, operating from a solitary table, orange boxes for filing cabinets and a shell-case for boiling tea, the CWGC representative started his monumental task. Through Normandy came all the new headstones - it was now estimated that 350,000 would be required and at first it was thought that it would take 15 years to complete the carving of them on the favoured Portland stone. A special factory was set up, with templates for each regimental badge and machines that could cut four headstones a day. The stones were to be set in concrete beams, four kilometers of which were needed to set the Normandy headstones alone. By 1948 spacious premises were acquired in Bayeux, the horticulturist was joined by an architect and a quantity surveyor, administrative and drawing offices were added and the old stables were converted into a garage, the garden became a plant nursery. As the number of staff increased a wing was converted into a hostel for single workers, run by a motherly French lady. The first Cross of Sacrifice of WWII was erected in Chouain cemetery. The first five Normandy cemeteries were built by the end of 1950 and by spring 1955 all eighteen had been completed, works and horticultural staff working in harmony to produce the pleasing and comforting cemeteries we see today. The Duke of Gloucester, then President of the Commission, unveiled the Bayeux Memorial in June 1955. The principal architect in Normandy was Philip Hepworth, a WWI veteran and Member of the Royal Academy Planning Committee for the rebuilding of London after the war. Hepworth was a draughtsman of the classical mould in the tradition of Lutyens and Baker - as can be seen in his gabled, barrel-vaulted entrance at Brouay and the watch-towers at Bény-sur-Mer. Hepworth always consulted the horticulturalists when designing his cemeteries, one of the most pleasing outcomes of the collaboration being the serpentine approach path at Banneville-la-Campagne (qv).

As time went on, staff were systematically reduced as the cemeteries were completed and machinery took over from manual labour. The policy of recruiting ex-Servicemen continued as far as possible, and for many years Ranville was attended by an officer who had landed there on D-Day and who helped bury some of his fallen comrades there. Sons and then grandsons of the original WWI gardeners continued the tradition, although today many local gardeners are employed. The cemeteries remain places of extreme peace and beauty, thanks to the dedication of the men who continue the standards set by the exceptional founder of this exceptional organisation, Fabian Ware.

The dedicated work of the Commission and its gardeners, who keep the cemeteries so beautifully, cannot be praised too highly. Please sign the Visitor's Book and record your comments. Your visit is appreciated by those who tend the cemeteries.

CWGC Cemeteries in Normandy, with numbers of burials/names

Banneville-la-Campagne	2,175	I2
Bayeux Cemetery	4,648	A11
Bayeux Memorial,	1,808	A10
Bény-sur-Mer Canadian	2,049	C25
Bretteville-sur-Laize Canadian	2,958	N4
Brouay	377	G22
Cambes-en-Plaine	224	H25
Douvres la Délivrande	1,123	C8
Fontenay-le-Pesnil	519	G8
Hermanville	1,005	D21
Hottot-les-Bagues	1,137	G9
Jerusalem (Chouain)	47	F7
Ranville	2,562	I17
Ryes (Bazenville)	979	B22
St Charles de Percy (still open)	800	L5
St Désir (+ 4 WW1)	598	I45
St Manvieu (Cheux)	2,183	G10
Sequeville-en-Bessin	117	G17
Tilly-sur-Seulles	1,222	F5

Plus many graves in local churchyards - look for the green CWGC 'Tombes de Guerre' sign at the cemetery entrance.

The local CWGC maintain the following private memorials:

15th Scottish Division

43rd (Wessex) Division

49th (West Riding) Division

15th Bn Dorsetshire Regiment

51st (Highland) Division

6th Bn AB Division

CWGC Website

The Commission holds records of 1.7 million Commonwealth War dead and its Enquiries Section can provide details of the place of burial or commemoration and where possible, directions to the cemetery or memorial. Enquiries are taken by letter, telephone or e-mail and, increasingly, searches can also be made using the online Debt of Honour Register at www.cwgc.org searching by name or cemetery.   The facilities of this incredible service are continually growing. A teaching resource, 'Remember me – echoes from the lost generations', with seven units, is now available. Website: www.cwgc.org/eduction

Head Office: Commonwealth War Graves Commission, 2 Marlow Road, Maidenhead, Berks SL6 7DX , UK. Tel: +(0) 1628 634221. Fax: +(0) 1628 771208. Website: www.cwgc.org E-mail: Casualty & Cemetery Enquiries: casualty.enq@cwgc.org.

Area Office in France: rue Angèle Richard, 62217 Beaurains, Tel: +(0)3 21 21 77 00. Fax: +(03) 21 21 77 10. **E-mail:** france.area@cwgc.org.

Local office: Tel: +(0)2 31 51 99 85   E-mail: steve.arnold@cwgc.org.

JOINT CASUALTY & COMPASSIONATE CENTRE (JC&CC) have now taken over from MOD PS4(A)NWG the handling of remains of service personnel where there is any likelihood of an identification, liaising with local embassies and CWGC, using case files and other appropriate researches. If families are traced their wishes are paramount as to the form of reburial.

Contact: Sue Raftree, RAF Insnsworth, GL3 1HW. Tel: +(0)14522 712612, ext 6303. E-mail: hstoricso3.jcc@innsworth.afppa.mod.uk General MOD website.

POLISH CEMETERY/BURIALS

The poignant Polish cemetery at Grainville-Langannerie, on the N158 south of Caen, contains 650 burials. It is maintained by the French Ministry of Anciens Combattants, rue de Bercy, *Paris 12.*

There are also Polish burials in Bayeux (25), Ryes (1), Douvres-la Délivrande (1), Ranville (1) and Banneville-la-Campagne (5). See the CWGC listing above.

VOLKSBUND DEUTSCHE KRIEGSGRÄBERFÜRSORGE
(The German War Graves Welfare Organisation)

The organisation is similar in function to the Commonwealth War Graves Commission and the American Battle Monuments Commission in that it maintains the war cemeteries and memorials to the German dead from World War I onwards. In 1956, the organisation, with the help of volunteer students, started re-interring the German war dead, then buried in 1,400 sites in Normandy, into the six large cemeteries which exist today.

La Cambe is described in detail on Itinerary Two above. Other German cemeteries in Normandy are:

Champigny-St André, between Evreux and Dreux, 19,795 burials

Huisnes-sur-Mer, near Mont St Michel, 11,956 burials

Marigny-la-Chapelle, near St Lô, 11,169 burials

Orglandes, near Valognes, 10,152 burials

St Désir-de-Lisieux, 3,735 burials

There are also German burials in many CWGC Cemeteries.

Contact: *Volksbund Deutsche Kriegsgräberfürsorge*, Werner-Hilpert-Strasse, 2, D-34112 Kassel, Germany. Tel: +49 (0)1805 7009 99. E-mail: info@volsbund.de Website: www.volsbund.de

Database at German Cemetery, la Cambe.

A wonderful facility exists at the Information Centre outside the German Cemetery at la Cambe. There is a freely available computer with a database containing the place of burial of all soldiers, sailors, airmen and others buried in war cemeteries in Normandy.

ORGANISATIONS FOR EX-SERVICEMEN AND REMEMBRANCE

THE AMERICAN LEGION

They also have information about the many strong American divisional and other ex-servicemen's associations. Head Office: PO Box 1050 Indianapolis, IN 46206, USA. Website www.legion.org French Office: 49 rue Pierre Charron, Paris 8ième, France.

AIRBORNE ASSAULT NORMANDY TRUST

A trust to preserve the history of 6AB's assault into Normandy. Membership open to veterans and interested associate members. Regimental Headquarters, The Parachute Regiment, Browning Barracks, Aldershot, Hants, GU11 2BU, UK. curatorairbornemuseum@btconnect.com

D-DAY AND NORMANDY FELLOWSHIP

The President is Vice Admiral Sir Geoffrey Dalton, KCB. **Contact:** Pat and Don Valler, Hon Sec and Reunion Organiser respectively, at 17 Clarence Road, Southsea, Hants PO5 2LG. Tel: 02392 732992. E-mail: valler@persim.freeserve.co.uk Website: www.DDNF.org.uk

THE NORMANDY VETERANS' ASSOCIATION

The Association was formed in April 1981 and by 1994 there were eighty-nine active branches, including international branches in France (Normandy), Holland, Belgium, New Zealand, Nova Scotia, Australia and West Germany. The members of the 68th branch, 'Calvados', fought with the Maquis. Representatives from the ten British regions form a national council. The current President is Major-General T.A. Richardson, CBE, MBE and the Duke of Gloucester, KCVO, is the Royal Patron. The Association has its own chaplain and national standard. Parades and services are held each year on the Sunday after 6 June and the Association parades on Remembrance Sunday at the Cenotaph. Some branches still run pilgrimages to Normandy each 6 June. The purpose of the Association is 'comradeship' and membership is open to all who took an active part in the assault on the beaches of Normandy, including all Auxiliary Services, WRENS, Nursing Services, ENSA and NAAFI. The Normandy Veterans, together with the D-Day and Normandy Fellowship (qv), commissioned Vivien Mallock (qv) to sculpt the statue of Field Marshal Montgomery at Colleville-Montgomery and contributed to the one at Portsmouth.

Contact: The Hon Gen Secretary is Capt Peter Hodge, RN, DMS. Tel: 0117 935 8081.

However it is advisable to contact your local branch for information, most of which now have good websites found by 'googling'.

ROYAL BRITISH LEGION

Their Pilgrimage Department arranges pilgrimages for war widows and families to CWGC cemeteries in Normandy. Their head office is RBL, Pall Mall, London SW1 and the Pilgrimages Department, run for many years by the enthusiastic Piers Storie-Pugh, is at the Royal British Legion Village, Aylesford, Kent ME20 7NX. Tel: 01622 716729, as is their tours department which also runs battlefield tours. www.poppytravel.org.uk.

COMITE DU DEBARQUEMENT (D-Day Commemoration Committee)

After the landings, the first 'Sous-Prefet' to be appointed in France was Monsieur Raymond Triboulet, OBE. He operated from Bayeux, the first French city to be liberated, and became Ministre des Anciens Combattants in 1955. He was also appointed Chairman of the '*Comité du Débarquement*', set up in May 1945, which is dedicated to preserving the sites and the memory of the invasion and the landing beaches. The *Comité* is responsible for the siting of ten '*Monuments Signaux*' (qv) - great stone markers commemorating the landing at, or Liberation of, Bénouville, Ouistreham-Riva-Bella, Bernières, Graye, Port-en-Bessin, St Laurent, Les Moulins (St Laurent), Isigny, Carentan, St Martin de Varreville and Ste Mère Eglise, as well as other memorials.

It also set up, or supports, the museums at Arromanches, Ste Mère Eglise, Cherbourg, Ste Marie-du-Mont (UTAH), Ouistreham, Tilly-sur-Seulles, Merville Battery the new Pegasus AB *Mémorial* Museum, and the *Mémorial* Museum at Caen. The *Comité* liaises with British regimental and ex-servicemen's associations to participate in ceremonies of remembrance in Normandy. On 1 October 1999 Monsieur Triboulet (who died in 2007) was succeeded as President by Admiral (2S) Christian Brac de la Perrière. Head office is at 4 rue du Bienvenu - BP 43402 Bayeux. **Contact:** Mme Lilian Bouillon-Pasquet. Tel: +(0)2 31 92 00 26. E-mail: debarquement2@wanadoo.fr

NORMANDIE MEMOIRE.

For the 60th Anniversary a sub-committee was formed, *Normandie Mémoire* 44, to co-ordinate the commemorative events with the same President as The *Comité du Débarquement*. It has now grown into an influential organisation which seeks to raise the standards of the many D-Day and battle for Normandy Museums in the region. A small but active and dedicated team under director Frédérique Guerin has as its aim to enhance the region's cultural, educational and tourist resources by organising, co-ordinating and promoting the operation and development of sites, museums and events that are linked to D-Day and the Battle for Normandy, to assure the historical verity of evocations of the battles and to encourage the deepening of historical and museum research.

It has an informative website: www.normandiememoire.com which offers a mine of information to prepare your visit to Normandy: videos, webcams, detailed descriptions of D-Day museums as well as events, commemorations, festivals and the complete history of D-Day and the Battle for Normandy.

Contact: the infectiously enthusiastic Sandy Cordone. Tel: +(0)2 31 94 80 26. E-mail: info@normandiememoire.com

THE SOUVENIR JUNO COMMITTEE

This committee was the inspiration of its Founder, M. Bernard Nourry. Current President is Monsieur Le Baron, Robert Mesnil, Cintheaux. Tel: +(0)2 31 51 55. E-mail: marielouiselebaron@wanadoo.fr Website www.france-canada.info

Its main aim is 'to perpetuate the memory of the liberation fight in June, July and August 1944, to worship the memory of the Canadians fallen dead on our ground during this time'.

Sixty *Communes* on the Canadians' liberation route have joined the Association and many of them have erected memorials with the date of their liberation and the name of the Canadian unit which liberated them. The Committee is extremely active, conducting 35 ceremonies of remembrance in the year 2007/8 alone, including the inauguration of many *steles*, most importantly a Canadian Memorial in Falaise.

Three itineraries have been marked with, at the entrance to the *Communes*, a red-on-white Souvenir Juno road sign carrying a Maple Leaf.

Route 1	Route 2	Route 3
Gray/Bernières	St Aubin/Courseulles	Caen
Reviers	Bény	Fleury
Fontaine-Henry	Tailleville	St André-sur-Orne
Thaon	Basly	St Martin-de-Fontenay
Bretteville l'Org	Anguerny	May-sur-Orne
Rosel	Anisy	Fontenel-le-Marmion
Rots	Villons le Buissons	Laize-la-Ville
Bretteville-sur-Odon	Cairon	Cintheaux
Putot	Buron	Soumont
Norrey St Contest	Authie	Potigny
Baron-sur-Odon	Carpiquet/Louvigny	

FRANCO-AMERICAN 9th US AIRFORCE NORMANDY AIRFIELDS ASSOCIATION

The dedicated founder was the assiduous researcher Madame Beatrice Bouvier-Muller who in liaison with American archivists, veterans and local participants of the Landings and Battle for Normandy, identified and marked, all the 9th USAAF 1944 airstrips in Normandy. They are (starting from Cherbourg, progressing towards Bayeux):-

A23	-	Querqueville (D45. North-west of Cherbourg)
A15	-	Cherbourg Airport. (D901. Near Maupertus)
A7	-	Fontenay-sur-Mer (D14-D214)
A24	-	Bénouville (D126)
A6	-	Beuzeville (D17/D115)
A8	-	Picauville (D69. North of Les Buts Dores)
A25	-	Bolleville (D903)
A14	-	Nr Coigny (D223/D138. North-east of Château de Franquetot)

A20	-	Lessay (D900. Near Aerodrome)
A26	-	Gonfreville (D140. Between Gorges and Gonfreville)
A17	-	Méautis (D443/D223)
A16	-	Brucheville (D424)
ELS	-	UTAH Beach, Pouppeville
A10	-	Les Veys (N13/D89)
A11	-	St Lambert (D19. Neuilly-la-Forêt)
A18	-	Le Dezert (N174. Near St Jean-de-Daye)
A3	-	Cardonville (D119/D199A)
A2	-	Cricqueville en Bessin (D194. La Grande Lande)
		La Cambe (Les Vignets)
A4	-	Longueille (Off N13)
A1	-	Englesqueville la Percée (seashore path above D514)
ELSA21	-	OMAHA Beach (Off D517. Les Moulins)
A22	-	Russy (West of D97. Château Rouge)
A13	-	Nr Vaucelles (N13)
A5	-	Cartigny-Epigny (Small road above D15)
A9	-	Le Molay Littry (D145/D191)
A19	-	Couvains (D92/D448)
A12	-	Lignerolles (Below D13)

The Association was also responsible for locating at Tournières General Eisenhower's 'First Command Post on the European Continent'.

Contact: President, M. D'Aigneaux, Tel: (0)2 33 21 22 91 or Communité de Commune de Montebourg. Tel: + (0)2 33 95 41 50

WINGS OF VICTORY OVER NORMANDY ASSOCIATION

An organisation started and researched by the dedicated Jacques Bréhin (and continued by his son Michel, Tel: (0)2 31 80 84 79) inspired by his contact with the downed British Pilot, Peter Roper, in June 1944, and supported by the RAFA and the *Comité du Débarquement*. Their most important achievement is the striking memorial in Noyers Bocage (designed by M. Triboulet) to the 151 Typhoon pilots killed in Normandy, May-August 1944. In 1994 the names of the pilots were added. Airstrip/Squadron markers are in the following Communes (with road numbers in brackets):

Bazenville	-	B-2 Airstrip. Plaque on cemetery (D87)
Bayeux Museum	-	Plaque
Bény	-	B-4 Airstrip, 401, 402, 422 Squadrons RCAF (D79)
Cheux	-	Plaque to Wing Commander Baker (D70)
Cully	-	B-6 Airstrip, 181, 182 Squadrons (D158)
Lantheuil	-	B-9 Airstrip, Memorial in *Mairie* RCAF (D93)
Le-Fresne-Camilly	-	B-5 Airstrip, Plaque (D22)
Longues Batterie	-	Airstrip B11
Martragny	-	Memorial to 438, 439, 440 Squadrons RCAF (D82)

Noyers Bocage	-	Typhoon Memorial, (designed by M Triboulet and costingover £55,000), Plaques to 151 Pilots (D875)
Ste Croix-sur-Mer	-	B-3 Airstrip Memorial & Plaques to 146 Wing/340/341 Free French Squadrons (D112A)
Sommervieu	-	B-8 Airstrip (D12)

Monsieur Bréhin also researched the crash site of Pilot Officer Donald William Mason, Royal Australian Air Force, died 18 June 1944, and in March 1993 his body was re-interred at St Charles de Percy. The intact engine of his plane is the museum at Tilly-sur-Seulles. In 2001 a plaque was erected to Flight Lieutenant Roy Crane (Honorary President of the Association, succeeding Monsieur Triboulet) in Mesnil-Hubert-sur-Orne (D25) where his plane was brought down in 1944 and dug up in 1991. During WW2 666 typhoon pilots were killed, average age 23. The Association continues to locate crash sites and make contact with pilots' relatives from the UK, Canada, Australia and New Zealand. Plaques and memorials are then erected in their memory. See the website: www.asavn.net President's e-mail: president@asavn.net M Jacques Bréhin was awarded the Australian Medal in 2007 for his work.

MEMOIRE, LIBERTE, CITOYENNETE (MLC) FOUNDATION

Ancien Combattant Yves Hue, with connections with many Veterans' Associations, started an Association based in the *Mairie* of Bayeux whose main goals are to perpetuate memory, encourage respect and civic virtues and to preserve a fragile peace. As part of the Normandy 60th Anniversary programme, the Association actively encouraged the participation of young people in planting Sequoia trees, the symbol of the Anniversary commemorations, together with small 0.80m high white Memorials with a Plaque bearing the logo of the Association. Conceived with the help of teachers and pupils of the Laplace Lycée at Caen, it shows an Arc de Triomphe with the eternal flame burning and above it the statue of Liberty. What about the British and Canadians, one might ask?

Some 60 Memorials have been placed in Calvados, La Manche, the Orne and the Eure.

Contact: M Yves Hue, 4 rue de la Vergée, 14740 St Manvieu Norrey. Tel: +(0)2 31 80 70 38. E-mail YvesHue@wanadoo.fr

GUILD OF BATTLEFIELD GUIDES

When we began our touring company over 30 years ago we were the first and only company running such tours. Since then battlefield touring has proliferated, with a wide variation in the quality of guiding. In 2002 Maj Graeme Cooper, a devotee and battlefield guide of the Napoleonic period, determined that a 'kite standard' should be created validating the capabilities of those who offered their services as guides. The Guild was duly launched on 28 November 2003 with Prof Richard Holmes as its Patron and the authors as Honorary Members. Its aim is to analyse, develop and raise the understanding and practice of Battlefield Guiding. It has since gone from strength to strength and the badge awarded to successful validation applicants is a mark of excellence and quality.

The Guild has a magazine and regular events, the highlight being the Annual Dinner Weekend in November.

Contact: Guild Secretary (and Founder), Maj Graeme Cooper, Coopers Court, Moreton, Ongar, Essex, CM5 OLE, UK. Tel: +(0) 1277 890214. E-mail: secretary@battleguides.org Website: www.battleguides.org

INTERNET

There is an increasing number of sites devoted to the Second World War. A search for the word 'D-Day' will bring up a large number of sites devoted to the Normandy Campaign. The most impressive is www.normandie441amemorie.com which lists memorials alphabetically by town/village with a photo. The webmaster is Patrick Corvé who works closely with *Normandie Mémoire* 44 (qv).

The coveted and respected Badge of an accredited Guide of the Guild of Battlefield Guides.

Monument to Non-violence, Caen Mémorial.

TOURIST INFORMATION
The Channel Crossing/Driving to Normandy

Cherbourg is the most convenient port of arrival from the UK for the American Beaches, Caen for the British/Canadian. Whichever route you choose your overall journey will take the best part of a day though there are overnight ferry services.

Poole/Portsmouth-Cherbourg
Brittany Ferries: Reservations/Prices/Sailing Times - Tel: 08705 360360. www.brittanyferries.com

Portsmouth-Caen. From Continental Ferryport off the M27 Motorway.
Crossing Time 6 hours daytime, approx 7 hours overnight. Cabins/Commodore Class/Reclining Seats available. New Rapid Service, Fri, Sat, Sun, March-Nov. Crossing time 3 hours 45 minutes.
   The ferry actually arrives at the Port of Ouistreham (qv). Then take the D514 to Caen (approximately 10 minutes).

Poole-Cherbourg. From the Terminal off the B3068 from the A35 (avoiding the lifting bridge).
Crossing Time 4 hours 30 minutes daytime, approx 6 hours overnight. Cabins/Club Class Reclining Seats available. New Condor Express service. One crossing, 0730 out, 1130 return. Crossing time 2 hours 15 minutes.

Portsmouth-Cherbourg. New Normandy Express service. Crossing time 3 hours.

Dover-Calais
Driving time Calais to Normandy around 4 hours
P & O/Stena Line. From Eastern Docks, Dover. Reservations/Prices/Sailing Times - Tel: 08716 646464. Website: www.poferries.com
Crossing Time - 75 minutes. Club Class available.
SeaFrance Ltd. From Eastern Docks, Dover. Reservations/Prices/Sailing Times - Tel: 0871 423 7119. Website: Crossing Time - 90 minutes. Club Class available.
Eurotunnel. From Eurotunnel Passenger Terminus, Folkestone-Cheriton.
Reservations/Prices/Sailing Times - Tel: 08705 353535. Website: www.eurotunnel.com
Crossing Time - 35 minutes. Club Class available.

The Ferry Travel Club offers good prices on Cross-Channel fares. Tel: 01304 213533. Website: www.ferrycheap.com

Travel Advice
If you live in the south-east you may find it quicker and more convenient to make the **Dover-Calais** crossing or to use the **Tunnel**. The 4 or so hour drive is now almost entirely on motorways and is well-signed. Key words to look for on signs from Calais/The Tunnel are, in journey order: A16/A26 Paris, A16/A26 Boulogne, A28 Rouen, A29 Caen. Most motorway sections are toll roads. You may use your credit card or set aside sufficient cash.

Some have a British flag with ticket push buttons/payment booths on the right.

The Ponts de Tancarville and de Normandie are toll bridges. The Pont de Brotonne is not. Recommended Maps: Blay Foldex Normandie No. 103 1/200,000 – 1cm + 2kms, then **Major & Mrs Holt's Battle Map of the Normandy D-Day Landing Beaches**. A free map of the SANEF motorways from Calais-Cherbourg may be obtained at the toll booths showing exits, motorway service stations.

It is advisable to keep your tank topped up with fuel as off the main routes petrol stations are few and far between and have short opening hours. There is an increasing use in petrol stations (especially at motorway stops) of chip and pin cards.

It is advised to keep within the signed speed limits. The French traffic police are very strict and can impose significant on the spot fines for speeding and other infringements. For instance from 1 October 2008 on the spot fines of between €90 and €135 may be imposed for not carrying a reflective jacket and a warning triangle. Drink-driving is also severely penalised. It is advisable to carry your motor insurance certificate with you.

Attractions of Normandy/action before you leave

The old Province of Normandie is divided into administrative *Départements*, two of which include the sites of the June 1944 Landings:

• **CALVADOS.** Its capital is Caen, while Bayeux is the main town of the area known as the Bessin. It includes the British Airborne actions (e.g. Merville Battery, Pegasus Bridge), GOLD, JUNO, SWORD and OMAHA BEACHES and Pointe du Hoc. It has beautiful sweeping sandy beaches and abounds with restaurants serving local specialities: fish and seafood, cider and the fiery liqueur which bears the *Département*'s name, Pont l'Evêque and Livarot cheeses, creamy sauces and crêpes.

• **LA MANCHE.** Its capital is St Lô, Cherbourg its main port. It includes UTAH BEACH and the American Airborne actions at Ste Mère Eglise. Famous for its studs for trotting horses, Isigny butter and caramels, Petite Ste Mère Eglise cheese and similar apple and seafood products.

The area abounds with theme parks, non-military museums, cultural and fun festivals, all of which add up to a very popular holiday area - not only with British and American veterans, but also with French holiday makers, especially from Paris, which is a short, easy journey away. It is, therefore, very important to book hotels or camping sites in advance during the busy summer season, which lasts from June to early September.

• **Contact the French Government Tourist Office**
Obtain a copy of their current Reference Guide for the *Traveller in France* from them at 178 Piccadilly, London, W1V OAL, Tel: 09068 244123. E-mail: info@mdlf.co.uk Website: www.franceguide.com. It contains up-to-date practical advice on *everything* the visitor to France needs to know.

• **Phoning to the UK from France:** Dial 00 44, then drop the first 0 from your number
• **Phoning to Normandy from the UK:** Dial 00 33 2 followed by the local number.
• **Phoning from one number to another in Normandy:** Dial 02 followed by the local number.

• **Opening Hours**

Banks: 0900-1200, 1400-1600 weekdays (some close Mondays or Saturdays).
Post Offices: 0800-1900 weekdays. 0800-1200 Saturdays. Currency may be exchanged at main Post Offices. You may need your passport at smaller ones. Stamps are also available at *Tabacs* (tobacconists).
Shops: 0800-1200/1230. 1400-1700/1800. Larger shops may close on Sunday and even Monday. Small food shops normally open Sunday morning. Supermarkets are open till late.
Churches: Normally not visitable by tourists during services. Often kept locked with keys held at the local *Mairie*.
Museums: Many shut on Monday or Tuesday. Smaller museums have restricted opening hours from October to Easter. Generally open weekends.
Public Holidays: New Year's Day, Easter Monday, May Day (1 May), VE (8 May), Armistice Day (11 November), Christmas Day.
Electricity: Mostly 220-30 volts. Two pin, circular plugs. An international plug adapter is recommended.
Metric Measurements: 1 kilo = 2.2lb. 1 litre = $1^{1}/_{4}$ pints. 1 gallon = 4.5 litres. 1 kilometer = 0.6 miles.

Tourist Offices

Known as *Offices de Tourisme or Syndicats d'Initiative*, they are to be found in all towns of any size. Follow '**i**' for information signs. Most of the useful tourist offices for Landing Beaches tours are listed in this book in a **distinctive typeface** as they are passed on the itineraries. Important offices are:

Normandy Tourist Board: UK. For information on Normandy see their website www.normandy-tourism.org Tel: 0117 986 0386. Fax: 0117 986 0379. E-mail: normandy@european-marketing.co.uk
Calvados Departmental Office: 8 rue Renoir 14054 Caen. Tel: (0)2 31 27 90 30, Fax (0)2 31 27 90 35. E-mail: cdt@cg14.fr Website: www.calvados-tourisme.com
La Manche Departmental Office: *Maison du Département*, 50008 Saint-Lô. Tel: (0)2 33 05 98 70. Fax: (0)2 33 56 07 03. E-mail: manchetourisme@cg50.fr Website www.manchetourisme.com
These tourist offices will make hotel reservations, give information on local restaurants, events (e.g. festivals, sporting events, concerts, shows), places of interest (e.g. museums, markets, Calvados distilleries), guided tours and 'Routes'; *du Fromage* (cheese); *du Cidre* (cider); *des Moulins* (mills); *des Trois Rivières* (three rivers - l'Aure, la Drôme and la Tortonne), etc, all with well-signed itineraries.

Note that many tourist offices close during the French lunch hour other than in the high tourist season and/or in larger towns.

WHERE TO STAY/EAT

Where you intend to stay will dictate what it is possible to see if you only have a short time, because the driving distance from the western American beach to Ouistreham at the eastern end of the British beaches is over 60 miles and takes at least 1.5 hours without stops. Thus, if you are looking to make a short visit – say just one day – for the British beaches, it is best to stay between Caen and Bayeux, and for the American beaches between Bayeux and Cherbourg.

Riverside, Courseulles, with de Gaulle Memorial behind.

Hotels/Restaurants

Those sited conveniently along the itineraries are listed in a **distinctive typeface** with their phone/e-mail numbers and basic details.

N.B. Many French kitchens close firmly at 1400 hours after lunch, so it is advisable to start looking for a lunch stop by about 1230, especially outside the main tourist season or off the main tourist routes. Some Pizzerias, which now proliferate in France, may be open all day. A picnic is highly recommended when you are out for the day.

Lists are obtainable from the national or local tourist offices (see above). Book well in advance for busy holiday periods and in September when the Caen International Fair (*Foire de Caen*) takes place - check the precise dates with the tourist office. The area is rich in hotels, from basic 'sans étoile'; * simple auberge/pension/group hotels like **Etap**; ** comfortable, well-presented, smallish rooms, e.g. **Ibis, Campanile**; and *** good quality e.g. **Mercure, Novotel, Best Western** etc; **** very comfortable, well-presented; *** *L superb quality, often converted chateux, gracious public rooms.

Logis de France. A grouping of small, normally family run hotels, with good regional and 'home' cooking. Head Office (which will supply their current brochure) 25 rue Jean Mermoz, 75008 Paris, France (or from French Government Tourist Office).

Gîtes de France. Self-catering cottages, apartments, farms, often in rural areas. All have running water, inside loo, shower. (List available from Tourist Offices.)

Chambres D'Hôte. Bed and breakfast often in farms or cottages, sometimes in small châteaux.

Delicious light lunch at l'Accostage, Ouistreham.

Camping Sites. The area (especially along the coast and on inland farms) abounds with camping sites, from sophisticated (with showers and many other facilities) to basic. On some, caravans can be hired. Lists from national or local Tourist Offices.
(Lists available from Tourist Offices.)

Veterans/Entrance Fees
D-Day or Normandy battles veterans should not be required to pay entrance fees in official museums. They may, however, be asked to sign the museum's *Livre d'Or* (VIP Visitors' Book).

GUIDED TOURS OF THE LANDING BEACHES

* The **Mémorial at Caen** arranges guided day tours and tours which include accommodation, including a facility to meet and drop off at Caen or Bayeux railway stations. Tel: (0)2 31 06 06 45. On-line bookings at www.memorial-caen.fr
* '**NormandYours**'. Tailor-made tours by experienced bi-lingual local guide, Danielle Duboscq. Contact: Tel: (0)2 31 22 43 09/(33)6 86.67 59 17. E-mail: danielle-duboscq@wanadoo.fr Website: www.normandyours.com
* **DDA '1994 War Museum on Wheels' Tours** in authentic 1944 vehicles with expert guides. Contact: Dr J-P Benamou, Tel/Fax: (0)2 31 80 82 61. E-mail: benamou.jp@wanadoo.fr Website: www.ddaca.com
* **Normandy Sightseeing Tours**. Pick up points in Bayeux/Caen. Daily from May-Sept. Oct-April by prior appointment.
* **D-Day Landing Beaches Tours** in minibus, jeep, boat, plane or microlite. Pickups at hotels around Bayeux. Tel: (0) 2 31 22 75 80. Website: www.dday-tours.fr

NORMANDIE PASS

This useful Pass card may be purchased for €1 at 25 or so D-Day/Battle of Normandy museums in the region or throughwww.normandiepass.com. It will give you reductions of up to 50%.

ACKNOWLEDGEMENTS

Our sincere thanks go to all those who have assisted us in the compilation of this guide, notably Mme Liliane Bouillon-Pasquet, MBE, Secretary *Comité du Débarquement*; Sandy Cordone of *Normandie Mémoire*; Marion Turpin, Bayeux Bessin Tourisme; Elisabeth Chartois and Nathalie Doron of CDT Manche; Steve Arnold, CWGC; Paula Bauer at the Normandy US Cemetery; Nathalie Worthington Director, JUNO Beach Centre; Gen Robert Pascoe, Ox & Bucks; Peter Knox for information on the 51st Highland Div; Dr Jean-Pierre Benamou, President D-Day Normandy Academy; Maj Jack Watson, MC for information on Putot-en-Auge; Ray & Cristy Pfeiffer and Capt (Retd) Greg Street, Naval Order of the USA for information about the Naval Memorial at UTAH Beach; Mark Warby, 'Old Bill Newsletter'. As always our thanks to Danielle Duboscq of NormandYours, our 'rep' in Normandy and our publishers, Pen & Sword Books, for their support, in particular our designer David Hemingway.

INDEX

FORCES

These are listed in descending order of size, i.e. Armies, Corps, Divisions, Brigades, Regiments, then numerically and then alphabetically. More units are mentioned in Cemetery descriptions throughout the book. Entries which refer to **Memorials are emboldened***.*

MEMORIALS/MONUMENTS/PLAQUES BY TOWN AND VILLAGE

In addition to those listed below many roads, squares etc are named as memorials to individuals and units who took part in the Landings and the Battle of Normandy.

GENERAL INDEX

MUSEUMS/PRESERVED BATTERIES/VISITOR CENTRES

WAR CEMETERIES